Enterprise and
National Development

ENTERPRISE
AND
NATIONAL DEVELOPMENT

ESSAYS IN CANADIAN BUSINESS
AND ECONOMIC HISTORY

Edited by

GLENN PORTER

AND

ROBERT D. CUFF

HAKKERT

TORONTO

1973

A.M. Hakkert Ltd.
554 Spadina Crescent
Toronto, Ontario M5S 2J9 Canada

Glenn Porter
HARVARD UNIVERSITY

Robert D. Cuff
YORK UNIVERSITY

Preface

These essays deal with a wide range of important topics in the interaction of business, government, and society in Canada. Their value is two–fold. As careful explorations of Canadian history, they provide important insights into the Canadian past. But the nature of the problems to which they address themselves also makes them useful guides to the Canadian present as well. In the continuing debate over such enduring Canadian issues as the mainsprings of national identity, the impact of foreign influence on the Canadian economy, the search for economic growth, and the optimum relationship between federal and provincial governments in shaping national development, historical understanding becomes ever more vital. Contemporary questions have deep roots in the past, and though historical investigation will not yield definitive answers, it can provide meaningful perspectives. This anthology represents, we believe, a contribution to the process of generating those perspectives.

Our thanks go to the various persons who contributed to the publication of this volume. We wish to express our particular gratitude to the authors whose work appears here. We are also indebted to Alan Samuel of A. M. Hakkert, Ltd., whose cooperation was exemplary.

A final word is due regarding the provenance of these essays. The studies in this collection first appeared in a special issue of the *Business History Review* devoted entirely to Canadian history. With their authors' consent, they are reprinted here exactly as they appeared in that publication. The *Business History Review* has been published since 1926 by the Harvard University Graduate School of Business Administration and is copyrighted by the President and Fellows of Harvard College. The facts and opinions expressed in this volume are, of course, solely those of their authors and are not to be construed as those of the Harvard University Graduate School of Business Administration or the President and Fellows of Harvard College.

Contents

Enterprise and
National Development

By Glenn Porter

ASSISTANT PROFESSOR OF
BUSINESS HISTORY
HARVARD UNIVERSITY

Recent Trends in Canadian Business and Economic History*

Canadian history has traditionally received relatively little study outside Canada itself, despite the fact that the Canadian past is a fascinating and rich story indeed, one which has generated an admirable body of historical literature. And, as those interested in the history of business and the historical interaction of business and society would expect, within Canadian historiography there has traditionally been relatively little emphasis on business history[1] The publication of the present collection of essays has a twofold purpose — to increase, however modestly, non-Canadians' knowledge of Canadian history, and to extend the body of scholarly work devoted to Canadian business and economic history.

In recent years that body of scholarly literature has grown very considerably. This brief introductory essay will touch on only a few of the developments apparent in the last fifteen years or so and will attempt to place the studies in this collection in the perspective of some of those trends. This introduction makes no pretense at completeness of coverage, however, as a great deal of noteworthy work is excluded from consideration, including the numerous recent contributions in such fields as the history of Canadian labor, agriculture, immigration, demography, and economic geography. Business history, however, is conceived of very broadly here; it includes not only the history of business but also the interrelationships between business on the one hand and economic development, governmental policy, and social change on the other.

Business History Review, Vol. XLVII, No. 2 (Summer, 1973). Copyright © The President and Fellows of Harvard College.

* The author wishes to express his thanks to the following persons, who kindly read this paper and commented on it: Robert Cuff, Hugh G. J. Aitken, James P. Baughman, James H. Madison, and Ralph W. Hidy.

[1] Complaints about the lack of attention given to business history in Canada are common. See, for example, Alan Wilson, "Forgotten Men of Canadian History," in Canadian Historical Association, *Report, 1965*, 71–86; Peter B. Waite, "The Edge of the Forest," in Canadian Historical Association, *Historical Papers 1969*, 9; and J. M. S. Careless, "The *Review* Reviewed: Or Fifty Years with the Beaver Patrol," *Canadian Historical Review*, LI (March, 1970), 67.

Although the amount of attention given to business history in the Canadian context has not been great, it must of course be noted at the outset that much outstanding historical work on Canada has been organized around the well known foundation of the country's economic history, the so-called staples approach. Until relatively recently, Canadian economic history and even Canadian history as a whole were heavily influenced and unified by the powerful synthesizing force of the staples hypothesis and its broader offshoot, the economic interpretation of Canadian history known as the Laurentian thesis. The product of such scholars as W. A. Mackintosh, Harold Innis, and D. G. Creighton, those approaches envisioned Canadian economic development as the exploitation of a succession of staples (fur, forest products, wheat, energy sources, metals, and others) demanded by outside markets, and the economic growth generated by the resulting expansion of transportation, income, commercial networks, and investment.[2] Although the approach takes on somewhat different coloring in the hands of different scholars, a good, concise summary of the model was given by Duncan M. McDougall: [3]

> We begin with an exogenous increase in the demand for a Canadian export and some available excess capacity in the export sector of the economy. This increased demand for a Canadian export leads to increased incomes and, after a lag, to increased investment in the export sector. Through the multiplier, incomes are increased in the home production sector also. Increasing incomes lead to increased importation of goods and, in turn, to an increase in customs and excise revenues. The increased tax revenues encourage the federal government to embark on long-awaited development schemes. The deflationary effects of a continuing merchandise deficit are offset, or more than offset, by the inflationary effects of capital borrowing on the basis of the optimism engendered by the rising demand for exports and the rising revenues.

The staples idea has some parallels with W. W. Rostow's notion of leading sectors, but it is peculiarly appropriate to colonial or newly settled economies.[4] In M. H. Watkins' view, the staples model is

[2] Mackintosh's essay of half a century ago is usually considered the pioneer statement of the staples thesis ("Economic Factors in Canadian History," *Canadian Historical Review*, IV [March, 1923], 12–25), though Mackintosh was careful to state that his views had been influenced by the work of Frederick Jackson Turner and Guy S. Callender. Innis' voluminous and excellent studies brought the approach to full fruition. See, among many other possibilities, his *Fur Trade in Canada: An Introduction to Canadian Economic History* (Toronto, 1930); *The Cod Fisheries: The History of an International Economy* (Toronto, 1940); and *Essays in Canadian Economic History* (Toronto, 1956). Creighton's most influential book was *The Commercial Empire of the St. Lawrence, 1760–1850* (Toronto, 1937).
[3] McDougall, "Immigration into Canada, 1851–1920," *Canadian Journal of Economics and Political Science*, XXVII (May, 1961), 173.
[4] See R. E. Baldwin's essay, "Patterns of Development in Newly Settled Regions,"

"Canada's most distinctive contribution to political economy." Its influence has extended well beyond Canadian history, as demonstrated by Douglass C. North's important *Economic Growth of the United States, 1790–1860.*[5]

The explanatory strength of the staples model underlay the leading general interpretation of Canadian history since Confederation in 1867, the interpretation commonly known as the Laurentian thesis. In that synthesis, the commercial empire that arose along the St. Lawrence River formed the heart of the emerging Canadian nation. The unifying theme of Canadian experience after Confederation was the task of overcoming the barriers of geography and regionalism, a task of nation-building. In the decades following Confederation, the federal government pursued the set of interrelated goals which came to be called the national policies.[6] Building on the foundation of staples, those policies included the support of railroad construction, tariffs to encourage the growth of domestic manufacturing, liberal immigration and land settlement, and the forging of a nation along an east-west axis. Until relatively recently, both the staples model and the Laurentian thesis were widely accepted by students of Canada's past.

The overall picture presented by recent work, however, is one of the gradual erosion of that consensus, though the staples approach has managed to retain much of its strength. Despite the arguments by Kenneth Buckley that the staple theory was an inadequate framework through which to explain the course of economic development in Canada, historians have continued to rely heavily on it.[7]

Manchester School of Economic and Social Studies, XXIV (May, 1956), 161–179. A good theoretical view of the model is also available in M. H. Watkins, "A Staple Theory of Economic Growth," *Canadian Journal of Economics and Political Science,* XXIX (May, 1963), 141–158, reprinted in W. A. Easterbrook and M. H. Watkins, eds., *Approaches to Canadian Economic History* (Toronto, 1967), 49–73.

[5] Englewood Cliffs, N.J., 1961. In North's version of the approach, cotton was the staple acting as the engine of U.S. economic growth between 1790 and 1860.

[6] Often the entire set of policies is lumped together and described as the National Policy, though that term is also used to refer specifically to the policy of protective tariffs. Borrowing the distinction of John Dales, in this paper, "national policies" refers to the entire program, and "National Policy" only to tariffs. See Dales, "Some Historical and Theoretical Comment on Canada's National Policies," *Queen's Quarterly,* LXXI (Autumn, 1964), 297–316.

[7] Buckley, "The Role of Staple Industries in Canada's Economic Development," *Journal of Economic History,* XVIII (December, 1958). An important study whose evidence and conclusions tended to diminish somewhat the staples thesis was Vernon C. Fowke's *The National Policy and the Wheat Economy* (Toronto, 1957).

Two recent examples of scholarship that indicate the continuing strength of the staples model are Gordon W. Bertram, "Economic Growth and Canadian Industry, 1870–1915: The Staple Model and the Take-Off Hypothesis," *Canadian Journal of Economics and Political Science,* XXXIX (May, 1963), 162–184, and Kevin H. Burley, ed., *The Development of Canada's Staples, 1867–1939: A Documentary Collection* (Toronto, 1971). Burley argues (p. xiii) that "economic development in Canada between 1867 and 1939 . . . is largely a story of the successive exploitation of the country's natural resources with the aid of capital and labour obtained in the main from external sources."

Other models of economic development have been used, such as the one employed by N. H. Lithwick in his *Economic Growth in Canada: A Quantitative Analysis.*[8] The staples model, however, still remains, in the words of Easterbrook and Watkins, "the most persistent theme of Canadian economic historiography."[9] Indeed, it seems most unlikely that the staple products and industries will ever be pushed very far from the center of the stage because of their central importance in Canadian history from colonial times at least through the first quarter of the twentieth century.[10]

The broad economic interpretation of general Canadian history has fared much less well than the staples notion. Canadian scholars often note and usually lament the fragmentation of Canadian historiography that has perhaps been its most notable recent trend. Taking stock of the writing of Canadian history as the *Canadian Historical Review* began its second half-century, Craig Brown and Michael Cross assessed the shattering of the Innis-Creighton historiographical consensus and the absence of any coherent synthesis to replace it. "Where," they asked, "are the studies of new staples, of communications, of the relationship between man and the land?"[11] One of the principal architects of the earlier synthesis, D. G. Creighton, recently registered a gloomy and pessimistic analysis of these trends.[12] It seems accurate to say that recent Canadian historiography has manifested a certain sense of drift and disunity.

The decline of the earlier consensus is visible in the shifting historical assessment of several topics that relate closely to business history. An important example is the growing scholarly split over the once-revered national policies and their nineteenth-century prime mover, Sir John A. Macdonald. Those questioning the wisdom of the policies do so from two main perspectives. One group,

[8] Published in Toronto in 1967 (second edition, 1970). Lithwick uses a Cobb-Douglas model, though he points out the importance of staples.

[9] Easterbrook and Watkins, *Approaches to Canadian Economic History*, ix.

[10] As Hugh G. J. Aitken noted in his introduction (p. xi) to the reprint of Gilbert Norman Tucker's *Canadian Commercial Revolution, 1845–1851* (Toronto, 1964), the recent questioning of the staples approach has related primarily to the late nineteenth and the twentieth centuries.

Nigel Kent-Barber argued that staples are virtually an inescapable historical fact and therefore will play a leading role no matter what the methodology favored by a particular historian. He perhaps overstated the degree of acceptance of the staples approach by declaring that "la thèse a fait son chemin au point qu'il n'est plus ni thèse ni école: c'est la base *totalement acceptée* de l'histoire économique canadienne." Kent-Barber, "La Théorie du commerce principal chez MM. Creighton et Ouellet," *Revue d'histoire de l'Amérique française*, XXII (December, 1968), 403.

[11] Brown and Cross, "The Beginning of Year 51," *Canadian Historical Review*, LI (March, 1970), 2.

[12] Creighton, "The Decline and Fall of the Empire of the St. Lawrence," in Canadian Historical Association, *Historical Papers 1969*, 14–25.

examining the policies largely from the point of view of per capita economic growth, emphasizes the economic price Canada paid in its attempts to forge a nation in the face of internal divisions, geographic obstacles, and the continual political and economic threats posed by the expanding United States. Discounting the importance of the search for political and economic unity and sovereignty in Canadian history, such scholars as John Dales have indicted the national policies as "a dismal failure."[13] In this view, the railroads designed to bind the Dominion's provinces together were built hastily and at too great a cost; the insistence on an east-west transportation axis in the face of economic advantages to links with the United States was misguided. The tariff barriers, rather than fostering the growth of domestic industries, merely resulted in reducing the standard of living, restricting Canadian manufacturers to home markets, and thereby encouraging the most able business leaders to emigrate (usually to the United States).[14] The government's land, immigration, and transportation policies encouraged too rapid and uneconomic settlement of the West, according to this interpretation. Although Hugh Aitken's work on government and economic development in Canada did not explicitly question what he termed the "strategy of survival" pursued by those who governed first British North America and then Canada, he pointed to the "recurrent conflict between commercial advantage and national economic unity."[15] Carrying the theme of the costs of the struggle for economic unity and independence from the U.S. into the twentieth-century history of Canada, economist N. H. Lithwick noted the recent trends toward growing economic connections between Canada and the U.S. and summarized the main themes of this "school:"[16]

> This growing homogeneity of the economies has appeared to some Canadians to be a threat to the "national identity" of this country. To offset this, protection has been maintained, along with ownership-of-industry and similar gimmicks. Whether these measures will lead to a peculiarly Canadian type of growth is highly unlikely, given the similarities in tastes and technology, and the high degree of factor mobility. These doubtful benefits should be weighed very carefully against the cost, calculated in terms of lower real income, that Canadians are now paying for these policies. An integrated North American economy will

[13] Dales, "Some Historical and Theoretical Comment," 302. See also his *Protective Tariff in Canadian Development* (Toronto, 1966).
[14] *Ibid., passim.*
[15] Aitken, "Government and Business in Canada: An Interpretation," *Business History Review*, XXXVIII (Spring, 1964), 4–21. See also his "Defensive Expansionism: The State and Economic Growth in Canada," in Aitken, ed., *The State and Economic Growth* (New York, 1959), 79–114.
[16] Lithwick, *Economic Growth in Canada*, 4.

maximize income in both countries and our reading of the past suggests that attempts to delay it have but one result; that is, to impose a fruitless burden on Canadians.

In contrast to those who give economic growth paramount place in assessing the policies of Canadian governments, others view the goals of political and economic independence as most important. Criticism by the latter has focused primarily on Canadian policies in the twentieth century. Some, like Stephen Scheinberg in his article in this collection, are careful to distinguish between the initial decades of the national policies (when they apparently helped achieve economic independence) and the more recent decades (when the American influence became so great). Much of this controversy has revolved around the protective tariff, and virtually everyone is agreed that, whatever its intent, one of the results of the tariff policy has clearly been to create incentives for foreign firms to establish subsidiaries and branch plants in Canada to produce inside the protectionist barriers rather than exporting over them.[17] The debate over the tariff is an old one, and no doubt it will continue until the far-off day when a clearer understanding of the costs and benefits of foreign investment emerges and is widely accepted.

The current argument is, moreover, an indication of another possible reason why the Laurentian synthesis has declined — the earlier teleological vision of Canadian history as a progression toward the achievement of a unified nation has perhaps been blurred by the re-emergence of old divisions in Canadian society and the growing problem of U.S. economic and cultural influence.[18] In any case, the historical assessment of the national policies (especially the tariff) is far from completed, and many recent studies continue to find the policies effective and laudable, at least in the period before World War I.[19]

Perhaps as another aspect of the decline of the earlier national synthesis, regional studies have flourished in recent years. T. W. Acheson's excellent works on the Maritimes and York are models of sound local and regional studies that integrate businessmen and

[17] The literature on this emotional topic is enormous. See, among many possibilities, Harry G. Johnson, *The Canadian Quandary* (Toronto, 1963); Ian Macdonald, "Foreign Ownership: Villain or Scapegoat?," in Peter Russell, ed., *Nationalism in Canada* (Toronto, 1966), 178–190; A. E. Safarian, *Foreign Ownership of Canadian Industry: A Study of Company Policies and Performance* (Toronto, 1966); Kari Levitt, *Silent Surrender: The American Economic Empire in Canada* (New York, 1971); and Hugh G. J. Aitken, *et al.,* *The American Economic Impact on Canada* (Durham, N.C., 1959).

[18] The overtones of Creighton's "Decline and Fall" paper suggest that recent historiography's rejection of the Laurentian thesis reflects a decline of confidence in Canadian unity and purpose.

[19] See, for example, T. W. Acheson's excellent paper, "The National Policy and the Industrialization of the Maritimes, 1880–1910," *Acadiensis*, I (Spring, 1972), 3–28.

business developments into the general context of the locale or region.[20] Local businessmen's organizations have also received growing attention from such scholars as Douglas McCalla and Fernand Ouellet.[21] Regional differences and their relation to economic growth have been examined by Alan G. Green.[22] The strong regional differentials noted by Acheson (in this collection and elsewhere) in the social origins of the Canadian industrial elite of 1880–1910 underline the need for additional studies cast in a regional framework.[23] Significantly, four of the contributions in the recently published anthology on *Canadian Business History* (edited by David S. Macmillan) are community studies.[24] Alan Wilson's piece in the present collection considers the prospects and needs for work in the business history of the Maritimes.

If one may consider French-speaking Canada as a region, business and businessmen also played a significant role in the historiography of that area.[25] One of the most interesting conflicts in recent studies of French Canada specifically involved questions of the role of business leadership in economic development — the controversy over the causes of the economic problems of French Canada after the conquest by Britain in the Seven Years War. Building on the work of Maurice Séguin and Guy Frégault,[26] a group of French Canadian scholars centered in Montreal argued that the British conquest "decapitated" French Canadian society and subjected the *Canadiens* to economic domination by English-speaking businessmen who assumed economic leadership in Quebec after the con-

[20] *Ibid.*, and his "The Nature and Structure of York Commerce in the 1820's," *Canadian Historical Review*, L (December, 1969), 406–428. For another example, see G. Stelter, "The Origins of a Company Town: Sudbury in the Nineteenth Century," *Laurentian University Review*, III (February, 1971), 3–37.
[21] McCalla, "The Commercial Politics of the Toronto Board of Trade, 1850–1860," *Canadian Historical Review*, L (March, 1969), 51–67; Ouellet, *Histoire de la Chambre de Commerce de Québec, 1809–1959* (Quebec, 1959).
[22] Green, "Regional Aspects of Canada's Economic Growth, 1890–1929," *Canadian Journal of Economics and Political Science*, XXXIII (May, 1967), 232–245, and "Regional Inequality, Structural Change, and Economic Growth in Canada, 1890–1956," *Economic Development and Cultural Change*, XVII (July, 1969), 567–583.
[23] In addition to his essay in this collection, see Acheson's "The Social Origins of Canadian Industrialism: A Study in the Structure of Entrepreneurship 1880–1910," (Ph.D. thesis, University of Toronto, 1971) and his contribution in Macmillan, ed., *Canadian Business History*, 144–174.
[24] Gerald Tulchinsky's piece on the Montreal business community and J. M. S. Careless' paper on the business community of Victoria, British Columbia, are especially noteworthy.
[25] Three useful recent bibliographic essays on French Canadian economic history are: Albert Faucher, "L'histoire économique de la province de Québec jusqu'a la fin du XIXe siècle," in Fernand Dumont and Yves Martin, eds., *Situation de la recherche sur le Canada français* (Quebec, 1962); Cameron Nish, "Bibliographie sur l'histoire économique du Canada français: Textes manuscrits et imprimés," *Actualité économique*, XL (June, 1964), 200–209; and Robert Mandrou, "L'Historiographie canadienne-française: Bilan et perspectives," *Canadian Historical Review*, LI (March, 1970), 5–20.
[26] Séguin, "L'Agriculture et la vie économique des Canadiens, 1760–1850," (Ph.D. dissertation, University of Montreal, 1948); Frégault, *Canadian Society in the French Regime* (Ottawa, 1958).

quest. Portraying New France as a society whose bourgeoisie of merchants and entrepreneurs (mostly connected with the fur trade) had close commercial and financial ties with France, these scholars saw the conquest as a developmental disaster that drove that bourgeoisie from power and snapped the links with France. Since only a petit bourgeoisie of small retailers, traders, and a few men in the professions then remained, the *Canadiens* fell under the yoke of English-speaking entrepreneurs whose commercial connections were with London.[27] That interpretation was challenged by Jean Hamelin's important *Economie et société en Nouvelle-France* (Quebec, 1960) and by Fernand Ouellet's masterful *Histoire économique et sociale du Québec, 1760–1850* (Montreal, 1966).[28] These latter studies denied the key role of the conquest, arguing instead that there never existed in New France an indigenous bourgeois group disposed toward entrepreneurial leadership to achieve industrialization.[29] Ouellet's massively researched investigation found in the value system of the citizens of New France many of the characteristics attributed to French Canadian businessmen of the mid-twentieth century — a belief in individualism and personal enterprise, a strong attachment to family and religious values.[30] The debate over the conquest and the economic development of French Canada has continued, but all parties to the controversy affirm the importance of business history in resolving the issues.[31]

Against the background of growing attention to regional studies and the fragmentation of sweeping syntheses, most recent business history in Canada has continued to be done in the framework of studies of particular industries and firms. Many of those have,

---

[27] Michel Brunet is probably the leading exponent of the "social decapitation" view. See his *La Présence Anglaise et les Canadiens* (Montreal, 1958), *Les Canadiens Après la Conquête (1759–1775)* (Montreal, 1969), and "The British Conquest: Canadian Social Scientists and the Fall of the *Canadiens*," *Canadian Historical Review*, XL (June, 1959), 93–106.

[28] See also Ouellet, "Le Nationalisme canadienne-française: De ses origines a l'insurrection de 1837," *Canadian Historical Review*, XLV (December, 1964), 277–290, and Ramsay Cook, "Some French-Canadian Interpretations of the British Conquest," in the Canadian Historical Association, *Report, 1966*, 70–83.

[29] Hamelin declared (*Economie et société*, 30), "Le drame de la colonisation française c'est de n'avoir pu former une bourgeoisie canadienne-française assise sur l'exploitation rationelle des resources naturelles du pays."

[30] See Jean-Charles Falardeau, "L'Origine et l'ascension des hommes d'affaires dans la société canadienne-française," *Recherches sociographiques*, VI (January–April, 1965), 33–46; Norman W. Taylor, "French Canadians as Industrial Entrepreneurs," *Journal of Political Economy*, LXVIII (February, 1960), 37–52 and Taylor's "L'industriel canadien-français et son milieu," *Recherches sociographiques*, II (April–June, 1961), 123–150.

[31] For a look at the historiographical conflicts, see Cameron Nish, ed., *The French Canadians, 1759–1766: Conquered? Half-Conquered? Liberated?* (Toronto, 1967). Among the treatments of Quebec in the period after 1850, see Yves Roby and Jean Hamelin, *Histoire économique du Québec, 1851–1896* (Montreal, 1971), and Francois-Albert Angers, "L'évolution économique du Canada et du Québec depuis la confédération," *Revue d'histoire de l'Amérique française*, XXI (1969), 637–655.

understandably, focused on the staple industries and on that pillar of the staples approach, transportation. The oldest and surely the most studied Canadian staple was fur, and recent historiography has shown no slackening of interest in that trade. Because of its amazing longevity and its unique political and economic role in Canadian history, probably no single enterprise has received (or merited) as much investigation as the Hudson's Bay Company. E. E. Rich's massive, detailed *History of the Hudson's Bay Company, 1670–1870*, is surely as exhaustive an example of a "company history" as one could want.[32] Recounting the history of the North West Company (Hudson's Bay's rival which it eventually absorbed) as well, Rich's work added substantially to the earlier large literature on the fur trade. John S. Galbraith's *History of the Hudson's Bay Company as an Imperial Factor, 1821–1869* (Toronto, 1957) was an important contribution which emphasized the company's political role as an agent of the British empire in North America. Galbraith also argued that the company's success was the result of its superior commercial abilities rather than the product of its legal and political advantages. Another major study of business activity in furs was Paul Chrisler Phillips' two volumes on *The Fur Trade* (Norman, Okla., 1961), which considered the topic in the entire North American context.

Despite the volume and quality of literature on the commerce in fur, such as the studies by Innis, Rich, and Phillips, interest has remained strong. Much scholarly and popular energy continues to go into analyses of local and regional aspects of the trade, into biographies of leaders in the business, and into the major enterprises which made fur the first of the great staple industries.[33]

Transportation has, of course, long been seen both as the means of marketing and extending the staples and as the means of building a nation in a hostile environment. In the new edition of his *History of Transportation in Canada*, G. P. deT. Glazebrook concluded his preface with a restatement of transportation's place in the Laurentian thesis: "Always there has been the challenge of

[32] Rich, *The History of the Hudson's Bay Company*, 2 vols. (London, 1959), also published in 3 vols. (New York, 1961). Rich also wrote *Montreal and the Fur Trade* (Montreal, 1966) and *The Fur Trade and the Northwest to 1867* (Toronto, 1967).
[33] Provincial and regional historical journals have devoted in recent years a very substantial amount of space to the topic. Among other recent monographs and articles, the following should be noted: D. Geneva Lent, *West of the Mountains: James Sinclair and the Hudson's Bay Company* (Seattle, 1963); K. G. Davies, ed., *Letters from Hudson Bay, 1703–40* (London, 1965); Marjorie Wilkins Campbell, *McGillivray, Lord of the Northwest* (Toronto, 1962); *Aspects of the Fur Trade: Selected Papers of the 1965 North American Fur Trade Conference* (St. Paul, Minn., 1967); George Woodcock, *The Hudson's Bay Company* (Toronto, 1971); and J. F. Crean, "Hats and the Fur Trade," *Canadian Historical Review*, XXVIII (August, 1962), 373–386.

environment;" he noted, "always the task before a small population of finding — whether through rapids or mountains, past ice and blizzards — a route to the Canada of the future."[34]

Perhaps no form of transport was more important in that task of overcoming geography and linking the pieces of Canada together than the railroad, and interest in the history of the railroad industry remained strong in recent years. Several different methodologies have been in evidence. Various company histories of railways appeared, including G. R. Stevens' two-volume study of the evolution of the troubled railroads that eventually emerged as a nationalized system after World War I — the Grand Trunk, the Intercolonial, the Grand Trunk Pacific, Great Western, Canadian Northern, and others.[35] Stevens' exhaustive study closed with 1922, after the Canadian National Railways had been launched. Many additional investigations dealing with the CNR will doubtless be made, for as a result of agreements worked out early in the 1960s, the CNR has deposited voluminous records in the Public Archives of Canada and eventually will place all its archival materials there.[36] One of the components of the Canadian National Railways, the transcontinental Canadian Northern, received from T. D. Regehr a more sympathetic treatment than earlier scholars (especially Stevens) had given.[37] Regehr emphasized the Canadian Northern's relatively successful history in the pre-World War I era and suggested that the developmental, nation-building contributions of the company balanced its otherwise questionable achievements as a business enterprise. John F. Due's *The Intercity Railway in Canada*, one of the volumes in the "Canadian Studies in Economics" series, recounted the history of firms in that specialized form of transport from its origins in the 1880s, tracing the initial expansion of intercity railways and their decline since the 1920s as motor vehicles grew in importance. Several recent publications by Patricia E. Roy, including her study in this collection, have delineated the early history of the British Columbia Electric Railway.[38] Two of the

[34] Glazebrook, *History of Transportation in Canada*, 2 vols. (Toronto, 1964), I, xii. See also Glazebrook, "Confederation and Transportation," *Revista de Historica de América* (1968), 41–51.

[35] *Canadian National Railways* I. *Sixty Years of Trial and Error (1836–1896)* and II. *Towards the Inevitable, 1896–1922* (Toronto, 1960, 1962).

[36] See John C. L. Andreassen, "Canadian National Railway Records," *Business History Review*, XXXIX (Spring, 1965), 115–19.

[37] T. D. Regehr, "The Canadian Northern Railway: The West's Own Product," *Canadian Historical Review*, LI (June, 1970), 177–187.

[38] The Due book was published in Toronto in 1966. In addition to Professor Roy's article in this collection, see also her "Regulating the British Columbia Electric Railway: The First Public Utilities Commission in British Columba," *BC Studies* (Fall, 1971), 3–20, and her contribution in David S. Macmillan, ed., *Canadian Business History: Selected Studies*.

forthcoming volumes in the Macmillan Company's "Railroads of America" series (edited by Thomas Brewer and Richard Overton) are scheduled to deal with Canadian topics — W. Kaye Lamb's *History of the Canadian Pacific* and G. R. Stevens' *History of the Canadian National*. Journalist Pierre Berton's lively retelling of the story of Canada's much-studied pioneer transcontinental, the Canadian Pacific, recreated the building of that road. A short, sympathetic, company-sponsored treatment of the Canadian Pacific by J. Lorne Mcdougall carried the company's story up to 1966.[39] Harold Innis' early work on that road, *A History of the Canadian Pacific*, was reissued in 1971 with a foreword by Peter J. George of McMaster University.[40]

Professor George, in his foreword to the Innis book and in other publications, considered the building of the road in the light of the work of Robert W. Fogel and Albert Fishlow.[41] George's estimates of the private rate of return for the CPR in its first decade of operations indicated that the project was unprofitable from an economic point of view and therefore that government subsidies were necessary for the undertaking.[42] His investigations of the subsidies, however, showed them to be clearly excessive, at least on an *ex post* basis. That is, the subsidies can be seen after the fact to have been greater than needed to raise the private rate of return to the "normal" level. George leaves to others the determination of the amount of aid necessary *ex ante*. Although he did not rigorously test the proposition, he also suggested that the CPR was very likely constructed ahead of demand, that it was a premature enterprise.[43] No thoroughgoing effort has as yet been made to measure the social

[39] Berton's two volumes on the CPR (*The National Dream* and *The Last Spike*) were published in Toronto in 1970 and 1971 respectively. A one-volume version has recently been issued in the United States under the title *The Impossible Railway: The Building of the Canadian Pacific* (New York, 1972). Mcdougall's book was *Canadian Pacific: A Brief History* (Montreal, 1968).

[40] Published in Toronto, a reissue of the 1923 edition.

[41] Fogel, *The Union Pacific Railroad: A Case in Premature Enterprise* (Baltimore, 1960) and *Railroads and American Economic Growth: Essays in Econometric History* (Baltimore, 1964); Fishlow, *American Railroads and the Transformation of the Ante-Bellum Economy* (Cambridge, Mass., 1965).

[42] See George's important article, "Rates of Return in Railway Investment and Implications for Government Subsidization of the Canadian Pacific Railroad: Some Preliminary Results," *Canadian Journal of Economics*, I (November, 1968), 740-762. Lloyd J. Mercer's "Taxpayers or Investors: Who Paid for the Land-Grant Railroads?" *Business History Review*, XLVI (Autumn, 1972), 279-294, estimates the contribution of subsidies to the investment in the Canadian Pacific system.

Following Fogel's lead, George defined the private rate of return as the ratio of operating profits (gross earnings less working expenses) in a given year to the cost of investment up to and including that year. The CPR was initially unprofitable in the sense that the private rate of return was below the opportunity cost of capital (or the "normal" rate of return on alternative investments).

[43] Lorne Mcdougall, on an impressionistic basis, agreed, terming it "desperately premature." Mcdougall, *Canadian Pacific*, 1.

rate of return of the CPR, but George's work may hint at some further buttressing of Aitken's suggestion that the Canadian government often pursued policies that sought national political and economic unity at the expense of "commercial advantage," and of John Dales' and others' assaults upon the national policies.

Although railroad history has been perhaps most prominent, other forms of transport have also been examined by able investigators. William Kilbourn's *Pipeline*, a history of Trans-Canada Pipe Lines, recounted and analyzed the interaction of business and government in a modern transportation industry.[44] Just as political considerations (especially nationalism and fear of U.S. economic domination) had helped to determine the nature and routes of earlier transportation enterprises in Canada and in British North America, they played a strong role in the evolution of this undertaking, lending new strength to Aitken's generalizations about government's "defensive expansionism" in its economic policies.[45] Another transportation project that deeply involved Canada's huge neighbor to the south was the subject of William Willoughby's *The St. Lawrence Seaway*.[46] Numerous other studies have appeared in recent years on various aspects of water transport (including the shipping industry) and on air transport.[47] Since transportation plays such a significant role in almost all explanations of economic development, there surely will be a continuing, substantial interest in this important sector of Canadian history.

Another side of business and economic history which usually receives a thorough and able investigation is money and banking, and recent work on this aspect of Canadian history has been unusually rich. Business historian Merrill Denison's company-sponsored study of the Bank of Montreal was a useful addition to the history of Canadian banking, especially his first volume on the bank's evolution to 1841.[48] R. Craig McIvor's *Canadian Monetary, Banking, and Fiscal*

[44] Kilbourn, *Pipeline: Transcanada and the Great Debate — A History of Business and Politics* (Toronto, 1970).

[45] Aitken's ideas also were seconded by Margaret Prang in her article, "The Origins of Public Broadcasting in Canada," *Canadian Historical Review*, XLVI (March, 1965).

[46] Willoughby, *The St. Lawrence Seaway: A Study in Politics and Diplomacy* (Madison, Wis., 1961).

[47] Examples include: C. A. Ashley, *The First Twenty-Five Years: A Study of Trans-Canada Air Lines* (Toronto, 1963); J. H. Hamilton, "The 'All-Red Route,' 1893–1953: A History of the Trans-Pacific Mail Service between British Columbia, Australia, and New Zealand," *British Columbia Historical Quarterly*, XX (January–April, 1956), 1–126; H. M. Paint, "Sailing Days Down East," *Canadian Banker*, LXVIII (Spring, 1961), 113–121, and Paint's "Financing the Welland Canal," *Canadian Banker*, LXVIII (Summer, 1961), 59–68; Howard Pammett, "The Steamboat Era on the Trent-Otonabee Waterway, 1830–1950," *Ontario History*, LVI (June, 1964), 67–103; John P. Parker, *Sails of the Maritimes* (Halifax, 1960); and Louise Manny, *Ships of the Miramichi* (St. John, 1960).

[48] Denison, *Canada's First Bank: A History of the Bank of Montreal*, 2 vols. (Toronto, 1966, 1967).

14   ENTERPRISE AND DEVELOPMENT

Development (Toronto, 1958) provided a historical overview that focused on commercial banking. The spring, 1967 number of the *Canadian Banker* contained a noteworthy assortment of historical essays, particularly those by Ian Drummond, E. P. Neufeld, Lorenzo Hébert, and J. Harvey Perry.[49] Works on particular kinds of financial intermediaries and on banking and politics have been prominent in the journals.[50] E. P. Neufeld's important, recently published book, *The Financial System of Canada: Its Growth and Development,* is a most welcome addition to the existing literature.[51] Though one always wishes for more explorations of the interrelationships between the history of capital markets and financial intermediaries on the one hand and the process of economic development on the other, the overall worth and quality of recent work on this aspect of Canadian history has been impressive.

In other areas of business history, some useful and welcome additions have been made in recent years, though it cannot be said that the history of manufacturing or of general business functions such as marketing have received the attention given to transportation, financial institutions, or the role of government. Perhaps the most interesting work has come from scholars looking at developments in a broader framework than either the firm or the industry. Gordon Bertram's very important statistical work on the growth of manufacturing in the last century or so has provided historians with invaluable data that can help place industry histories in the context of the overall manufacturing sector.[52] Bertram himself led the way with some provocative generalizations about Canadian industry, especially his argument that the manufacturing sector's growth was well under way before the traditional date for the beginnings of rapid industrialization. In the process, Bertram joined the crowded ranks of those who saw in various countries a gradual process of growth rather than the sudden "take-off" hypothesized by Ros-

---

[49] *Canadian Banker,* LXXIV (Spring, 1967). The four essays mentioned were: Drummond, "Financial Institutions in Historical Perspectives," 150–58; Neufeld, "Canadian Financial Intermediaries — A Century of Development," 143–49; Hébert, "Les Banques en Canada en 1867," 83–95; and Perry, "Origins of the Canadian Bankers' Association," 96–114.

[50] See, for example, Ian M. Drummond, "Canadian Life Insurance Companies and the Capital Market, 1890–1914," *Canadian Journal of Economics and Political Science,* XXVIII (May, 1962), 204–224; Carol Lawrie Vaughn, "The Bank of Upper Canada in Politics, 1817–1840," *Ontario History,* LX (December, 1968), 185–205; and Francois-Albert Angers, "Le Financement des emprunts provinciaux et la Banque du Canada," *Actualité économique,* XXXVIII (January–March, 1963), 548–568.

[51] See also Neufeld's *Money and Banking in Canada: Historical Documents and Commentary* (Toronto, 1964).

[52] Bertram, "Historical Statistics on Growth and Structure in Manufacturing in Canada, 1870–1957," in J. Henripen and A. A. Asimkopulos, eds., *Canadian Political Science Association Conference on Statistics: 1962 and 1963 Papers* (Toronto, 1964).

tow.[53] Other important statistical work has been done by Gideon Rosenbluth on concentration in Canadian industry.[54] Perhaps the most welcome statistical arrival, however, was Urquhart and Buckley's *Historical Statistics of Canada*, covering the years 1867–1960.[55] Since most Canadian economic data, like those everywhere else, are collected by government, the publication of the *Historical Catalogue of Dominion Bureau of Statistics Publications, 1918–1960* [56] added considerably to the historians' bibliographical arsenal. The appearance of other studies in economics, such as Buckley's work on capital formation, Chambers' research on business cycles, and O. J. Firestone's contribution to the Simon Kuznets-inspired "Income and Wealth Series," have aided enormously in the expansion of aggregate economic data useful to business historians.[57] Such broad-gauged investigations have not been numerous; the great bulk of Canadian studies of interest to business historians has dealt with particular businessmen, firms, or industries.

A number of company histories of major Canadian firms have appeared in recent years, adding their contributions to the shelf of literature on business institutions. To his volume on the Molson brewing enterprise, Merrill Denison added a monograph on Ontario Hydro, a public enterprise.[58] In addition to his pipeline study, William Kilbourn published a good study of Stelco and its predecessors, *The Elements Combined: A History of the Steel Company of Canada* (Toronto, 1960). The work of O. W. Main and others extended historians' knowledge of the nickel industry.[59] E. P. Neufeld's *A Global Corporation* was a well-received look at one of Canada's major enterprises.[60] The appearance of more and more studies of multinational corporations (such as the Wilkins-Hill book

[53] See Bertram, "Economic Growth and Canadian Industry, 1870–1915: The Staple Model and the Take-Off Hypothesis," *Canadian Journal of Economics and Political Science*, XXIX (May, 1963), 162–184.

[54] Rosenbluth, *Concentration in Canadian Manufacturing Industries* (Princeton, N.J., 1957), and his "The Relationship between Foreign Control and Concentration in Canadian Industry," *Canadian Journal of Economics*, III (February, 1970), 14–38. See also Richard E. Caves and Richard H. Holton, *The Canadian Economy: Prospect and Retrospect* (Cambridge, Mass., 1959).

[55] M. C. Urquhart and K. A. H. Buckley, eds., *Historical Statistics of Canada* (Toronto, 1965).

[56] Ottawa, 1967.

[57] Kenneth Buckley, *Capital Formation in Canada, 1896–1930* (Toronto, 1955); Edward J. Chambers, "Canadian Business Cycles since 1919: A Progress Report," *Canadian Journal of Economics and Political Science*, XXIV (May, 1958), 166–189; and O. J. Firestone, *Canada's Economic Development, 1867–1953* (London, 1958).

[58] Denison, *The Barley and the Stream: The Molson Story* (Toronto, 1955), and *The People's Power: The History of Ontario Hydro* (Toronto, 1960).

[59] O. W. Main, *The Canadian Nickel Industry: A Study in Market Control and Public Policy* (Toronto, 1955), and John F. Thompson and Norman Beasley, *For the Years to Come: A Story of International Nickel of Canada* (New York, 1960). See also Main's essay in Macmillan, ed., *Canadian Business History*.

[60] Neufeld, *A Global Corporation: A History of the International Development of Massey-Ferguson Limited* (Toronto, 1969).

on Ford) [61] has notably increased the understanding of the opera-tions of large firms producing and competing in the Canadian en-vironment. Other monographs, often journalistic and aimed at the popular market, have also continued to be produced by and about firms and industries.[62] Biographies of businessmen, on the whole, have not yet been as much in evidence as one might expect, but there is a very varied array of recent monographs, journal articles, and autobiographical materials.[63] T. W. Acheson's group biographi-cal approach (in this collection) has few if any counterparts. The scholarly historical journals have, of course, continued to produce many articles about firms and industries, and many of those have been of very good quality.[64] There is plenty of secondary raw material awaiting would-be generalizers.

Raw material of other sorts has also increased significantly. The records of firms are not plentiful in Canada, but they are growing in availability.[65] The formation of the Business Archives Council of Canada may help to make the archival future brighter, though there are at present (if Alan Wilson's survey of the Maritimes is typical) significant unused archival materials pertaining to business. Bibli-ographic and reference aids of importance to business historians

[61] Mira Wilkins and Frank Ernest Hill, *American Business Abroad: Ford on Six Con-tinents* (Detroit, 1964).

[62] See, for example, Mary-Etta Macpherson, *Shopkeepers to a Nation: The Eatons* (Toronto, 1963), and Eric J. Hanson, *Dynamic Decade: The Evolution and Effects of the Oil Industry in Alberta* (Toronto, 1958).

[63] See, for example: James G. McGregor, *Edmonton Trader: The Story of John A. McDougall* (Toronto, 1963); T. W. Acheson, "John Baldwin: Portrait of a Colonial Entre-preneur," *Ontario History*, LXI (September, 1969), 153–166; Donald Swainson, "Business and Politics: The Career of John Willoughby Crawford," *Ontario History*, LXI (December, 1969), 225–236; J. M. S. Careless, "The Lowe Brothers, 1852–70: A Study of Business Relations on the North Pacific Coast," *BC Studies* (Summer, 1969), 1–18; Frederick H. Armstrong, "George Jervis Cooper: Pioneer Merchant of London, Ontario," *Ontario History*, LXIII (December, 1971), 217–232; and less substantial contributions such as Hugh Maclean's *Man of Steel: The Story of Sir Sandford Fleming* (Toronto, 1969), and Peter C. Newman's *Flame of Power: Intimate Profiles of Canada's Greatest Businessmen* (Toronto, 1959). Two recent autobiographical entries include: Frederick S. Mendel (founder of Intercontinental Packers), *The Book and Life of a Little Man* (Toronto, 1972), and Martin Nordegg (an entrepreneur in the Alberta coalfields), *The Possibilities of Canada Are Truly Great: Memoirs, 1906–1924* (edited by T. D. Regehr, Toronto, 1971).

[64] A sampling of these includes the following (not mentioned previously): W. D. G. Hunter, "The Development of the Canadian Uranium Industry: An Experiment in Public Enterprise," *Canadian Journal of Economics and Political Science*, XXVIII (August, 1962), 329–352; Keith Ralston, "Patterns of Trade and Investment on the Pacific Coast, 1867–1892: The Case of the British Columbia Salmon Canning Industry," *BC Studies* (Winter, 1968–69), 37–45; W. D. Whitham, "Les investissements américains et les origines de l'industrie pétrolière canadienne," *Actualité économique*, XLIV (January–March, 1969), 689–710; W. D. Whitham, "L'Industrie canadienne des pâtes et papiers," *Actualité économique*, XLV (July–September, 1969), 267–298; D. S. G. Ross, "History of the Electrical Industry in Manitoba," Historical and Scientific Society of Manitoba, *Papers*, series III, 20, 1963–64, 49–70; and Edward Phelps, "The Canada Oil Association — An Early Business Combi-nation," *Western Ontario Historical Notes*, XIX (September, 1963), 31–39.

[65] See John Hall Archer, "Business Records: The Canadian Scene," *American Archivist*, XXXII (July, 1969), 251–59, and Archer's piece in Macmillan, ed., *Canadian Business History*.

have proliferated in the recent past.[66] There are, in short, more and more opportunities for students of Canadian business history.

As the essays in this collection indicate, scholars are grasping many of those opportunities. Although the interrelationships between business and government have been extensively examined in the Canadian context, the article by Christopher Armstrong and H. V. Nelles on federal-provincial relations and the business community in Ontario demonstrates that the topic still has much to offer. Michael Bliss' piece on the anti-combines tradition, Stephen Scheinberg's contribution on tariffs and U.S. economic expansion in Canada, and Patricia Roy's paper on the management of an important transport enterprise all raise significant questions about a range of issues of business and public policies. Such questions as the role and impact of foreign-based managers in a branch-plant economy, the importance of provincial-federal differences over economic development, and the similarities and contrasts between business-government relations in Canada and other nations, all emerge as topics deserving further investigation. As disputes over the future role of Canadian developmental policies continue, an understanding of the historical evolution of domestic enterprise and of foreign involvement in Canadian business will be more important than ever. Regional studies seem assured of future interest, and the papers of T. W. Acheson and Alan Wilson surely constitute important contributions in that context. The relationships between business history and social history are clearly a favorite topic of current scholarly interest, and more work like Acheson's on the social origins of business leaders and the degree of mobility and openness in the business world will help to carry impressions about the business community's past onto firmer ground.

Several recent events, including the appearance of the present assortment of scholarly articles, point to the continuing interest in the business and economic history of Canada. An important milestone was the 1967 meeting of the Business History Conference in London, Ontario. That gathering drew many eminent historians, economists, businessmen, and others interested in this aspect of Canadian history; most of the papers delivered at the meeting dealt

---

[66] Especially noteworthy and laudable are: Robert S. Gordon, ed., *Union List of Manuscripts in Canadian Repositories* (Ottawa, 1968); W. D. Wood, L. A. Kelly, and P. Kumer, comps., *Canadian Graduate Theses, 1919–1967: An Annotated Bibliography Covering Economics, Business, and Industrial Relations* (Kingston, 1970); and the continuing appearance of the volumes in George W. Brown, ed., *Dictionary of Canadian Biography* (Toronto, 1966–). See also Robert W. Lovett, *American Economic and Business History Information Sources* (Detroit, 1971); Lorna M. Daniells, comp., *Studies in Enterprise* (Boston, 1957) and annual supplements in the *Business History Review*, 1959–1964; and Barbara B. Byers, *et al.*, *Early Canadian Companies* (Toronto, 1967).

with Canadian topics and were published as the *Proceedings of the Fourteenth Annual Meeting of the Business History Conference* (London, Ontario, 1967). The publication of the essays in David Macmillan's *Canadian Business History* (Toronto, 1972) gives further indication of the vitality of the field.

As historians build on the present foundations of Canadian business history, it may be hoped that other avenues of investigation will be opened. There is much need for comparative studies that examine the history of many firms, industries, businessmen, and business functions across Canada and over time. Although company studies still have contributions to make, it seems perhaps more urgent and more promising to have new, broad-ranging studies of such topics as the evolution of management, the history of marketing or production, the historical performance and consequences of firms controlled from abroad, the role of staples in a mature economy, government-business relations, and the connections between business activities and the building of communities, regions, and the Canadian nation as a whole. The greatest need in Canadian business history — as in business history elsewhere, and, indeed, in history in general — continues to be the need for interesting and provocative generalizations resting on good empirical bases. A country whose scholars produced such syntheses as the staples model and the Laurentian thesis may yet become the generator of new hypotheses and new directions in business history. And, since studies of business and economic history once formed the foundation for wide-ranging interpretations of the Canadian past, it is not beyond the realm of possibility that new work in those fields may again generate fruitful and exciting approaches to Canadian history as a whole.

By *Christopher Armstrong*
ASSISTANT PROFESSOR OF HISTORY
YORK UNIVERSITY
AND
H. V. Nelles
ASSISTANT PROFESSOR OF HISTORY
YORK UNIVERSITY

Private Property in Peril: Ontario Businessmen and the Federal System, 1898-1911*

❡ *Two opposing groups of business interests — large, internationally-oriented financiers on the one hand and local businessmen and small manufacturers on the other — engaged in economically-based political conflict over the proper nature of the federal system in early twentieth-century Canada. The national financial community proved unable to protect its conception of private property rights by legal and political means at the national level, and the resulting victory of provincial rather than federal control over property rights made possible the creation of a publicly owned hydro-electric system in Ontario.*

By the end of the nineteenth century, new forms of business organization in North America began to produce new demands upon the state from the business community. Professor Gabriel Kolko has argued that in the United States, "Progressivism was . . . the victory of big businesses in achieving the rationalization of the economy that only the federal government could provide." Central control of the economy removed regulatory functions from the hands of the "unpredictable" state legislatures to the safety of Washington. As a national business and financial community began to emerge in Canada at that time, its members attempted to do the same thing.[1] They failed. The decentralized Canadian federal

Business History Review, Vol. XLVII, No. 2 (Summer, 1973). Copyright © The President and Fellows of Harvard College.

* The authors wish to acknowledge the helpful criticism of their colleagues in the Department of History, York University, and of Professor J. M. Bliss of the University of Toronto.

[1] Gabriel Kolko, *The Triumph of Conservatism: A Reinterpretation of American History, 1900–1916* (Chicago, 1963), 284. Robert H. Wiebe also concludes that, "In all, the business community was the most important factor — or set of factors — in the development of economic regulation." *Businessmen and Reform: A Study of the Progressive Movement* (Chicago, 1962), 217. On the emergence of a group of financiers with national and inter-

system prevented escape from the volatile provincial level to Ottawa. In the province of Ontario, moreover, a publicly owned hydro-electric system was established over the objections of a powerful group within the business community, fearful of a general assault upon the rights of private property.

In that struggle to define property rights, businessmen discovered that Canada's federal system provided them with a number of different points of access to the political process. Under the Canadian constitution, the provinces retained jurisdiction over property and civil rights, a provision liberally interpreted by the courts. During the 1890s a series of constitutional cases clarified the extent of provincial power. In 1892 the Judicial Committee of the British Privy Council decided that the British North America Act had not been intended "to subordinate provincial governments to a central authority, but to create a federal government . . . , each province retaining its independence and autonomy." Three years later this view was extended to its logical conclusion with the finding that "the exclusive powers of the provincial legislatures may be said to be absolute." In the Fisheries Reference of 1898, the claim of the provinces to control all their lands and natural resources was sustained, and at the same time the argument that provincial powers might be abused by the confiscation of private property was summarily dealt with: "The supreme legislative power in relation to any subject-matter is always capable of abuse, but it is not to be assumed that it will be abused; if it is the only remedy is an appeal to those by whom the legislature is elected." [2]

The significance of these decisions may be gauged by noting that in the same year, 1898, the Supreme Court of the United States completed a process of constitutional reinterpretation on precisely the same issue and came to the opposite conclusion. The Fourteenth Amendment forbade the states from taking anyone's property without "due process of law." Previously, this phrase had always been construed in purely procedural terms. After the Civil War, however, the claim began to be advanced that due process had a

---

national interests, centered in Montreal and Toronto, see T. W. Acheson, "The Social Origins of Canadian Industrialism: A Study of the Structure of Entrepreneurship" (Ph.D. thesis, University of Toronto, 1971), *passim*.

[2] There is a vast literature on the development of the Canadian constitution. Canada, Senate, *Report Pursuant to the Resolution of the Senate to the Honourable the Speaker by the Parliamentary Counsel [W. F. O'Connor] Relating to the Enactment of the British North America Act* (Ottawa, 1939) reprints extracts from the first and third judgments quoted; see Annex 3, Case 10, *Liquidators of the Maritime Bank v. Receiver General of New Brunswick* (1892), 28–29, and Case 16, *Attorney General for Canada v. Attorney General for Ontario (Fisheries Reference)* (1898), 42–46. Lord Herschell's decision in *Brophy v. Attorney General for Manitoba* (1895) is quoted in W. P. M. Kennedy, *The Constitution of Canada* (London, 1922), 421.

substantive connotation as well, that it included the protection of vested rights. By 1898 the Court had accepted this, declaring that it had the authority to review all state legislation to see that it did not violate the sacred rights of private property in any "unreasonable" way. In the words of Mr. Justice Field, no longer would all property and business in a state be "held at the mercy of a majority of its legislature."[3]

Confirmation of the decentralized character of the Canadian federation could hardly have come at a more opportune moment for some groups within the business community. As the industrialization and urbanization of North America produced an ever increasing demand for the natural resources of the province, competition amongst promoters for the right to exploit these on favorable terms naturally intensified. Local businessmen and small manufacturers also began to resist efforts by the new aristocracy of financiers to monopolize such vital resources as hydro-electricity, upon which future industrial development depended.

Because businessmen constituted the dominant class in Canadian society, they assumed that the state should be organized to meet their needs. But these changes in the structure of economic life meant that different groups within the business community now seemed to have conflicting needs. Accordingly, the two groups (local businessmen and small manufacturers on the one hand, and large financiers on the other) relied upon different arms of the state to defend their competing interests. The responsibilities of the national financial community consisted not simply of mobilizing the savings of the country and restructuring its economy, but also — and perhaps more important — of organizing the necessary borrowings abroad. This group came to believe that the central government ought to use its regulatory power to stabilize the economy in accordance with their objectives, in part by controlling the behaviour of the provinces. Their adversaries, obedient to the dialectic of federal-provincial relations, turned to the provincial governments to attain their ends. Thus two different conceptions of the proper nature of the federal system emerged, each one depending upon the way in which the individual businessman perceived his place in the new corporate economy.[4]

[3] Alfred H. Kelly and Winfred E. Harbison, *The American Constitution, Its Origins and Development* (3rd ed., New York, 1963), 496–542. Field is quoted at 509. This represented a complete reversal of the position taken by the majority in *Munn v. Illinois* (1877), where Chief Justice M. R. Waite declared, "For protection against abuses by legislatures the people must resort to the polls, not to the courts." See Arthur S. Miller, *The Supreme Court and American Capitalism* (New York, 1968), 53.
[4] To some degree this begs the question of the precise connection between ideology and

The international obligations of the national financial community provide a key to understanding their determination in this matter. What was at stake in this conflict was both the power of the financial sector in the Canadian economy and its reputation in the capital markets of the world. The circumstances of the hinterland meant that the president of the Bank of Montreal could not occupy the same self-sufficient position in Canada's economy as the leading bankers in New York did in the United States. The Canadians had always to be sensitive — some would say oversensitive — to their relationship with the London metropolis. In a colonial economy, the recurrent nightmare of a nervous banker was a loss of confidence in London leading to a wholesale flight of capital.

Businessmen could seek assistance or protection from either level of government according to their needs. The diffusion of authority also made possible competition between private interests. Those who felt aggrieved by state intervention could try to recoup their position by playing off one level against the other. This produced federal-provincial conflict in which the two levels of government represented opposing economic interests. A consistent pattern soon emerged as different elements within the business community regularly sought help from different levels of government. Local business and manufacturing interests (along with certain other reformist pressure groups) came to rely upon provincial control of property and civil rights. The national financial community looked to Ottawa.

For example, in 1897 a group of Ontario lumbermen induced the provincial government to impose a manufacturing condition forbidding the export of pine timber cut on Crown lands unless it was sawn in Canada. This effective response to the retaliatory provision of the Dingley tariff demonstrated that the province's control of its lands and natural resources could be used to direct economic development regardless of federal trade policy. Financiers with national or international interests soon recognized the dangers which this posed for them. Urged on by the American-controlled International Nickel Company, which threatened to close down its Canadian mining operations altogether, the Wilfrid Laurier administration thwarted an attempt by the Ontario government to extend a similar manufacturing condition to nickel refining in 1901.[5] Be-

material interest. We hope to examine the question of whether these differing conceptions represented conflicting business ideologies through further empirical study of the behavior of entrepreneurs in the utilities field in Ontario.

[5] H. V. Nelles, "Empire Ontario: The Problems of Resource Development," in Donald Swainson, ed., *Oliver Mowat's Ontario* (Toronto, 1972), 189–210, and Nelles, "The Politics

cause the courts had refused to restrict the authority of the province over its property, these economic wars had to be fought out in the political arena in Canada. By 1901, however, it was not yet clear to what extent a provincial legislature would be permitted to violate the sacred rights of private property without provoking intervention by the central government on behalf of the injured parties. The next decade saw the resolution of this question with a clear victory for the supporters of the province.

REFORM AT THE PROVINCIAL LEVEL

The matter was brought to a head in Ontario by the rise of a local variant of Progressivism. The men who turned to Ottawa demanding protection and regulation of the developing national economy were stockbrokers, railroad promoters, corporate executives, and utilities magnates. They complained that the provincial government, acting at the behest of local merchants and manufacturers, was confiscating their property.

The businessmen who leaned most heavily upon the federal authorities were traction and utilities operators fleeing regulation at the local level and mining promoters hurt by new provincial regulations. In a resource-rich, rapidly urbanizing province, mines and utilities were the two most controversial forms of capitalist enterprise. Successful promotions generated enormous profits which seemed out of all proportion to the initial investment. The stock watering which characterized the organization of these companies and the manipulation which typified trading in their securities created resentments. Moreover, the monopolistic character of the utilities, their poor but expensive service, and their notorious public relations made them prime targets for attack. Finally, the concentrations of capital embodied in enterprises like the utilities in particular, rendered them the property of an exclusive, highly visible, and obviously favored group of men. That other businessmen depended upon the cheapness and efficiency of the services provided by this class of enterpreneurs only sharpened the conflict.

The thrust of reform, designed to eliminate these abuses, came largely from smaller businessmen who moulded popular resentment to their own ends. Only in mining and hydro-electricity did this

---

of Development: Forests, Mines and Hydro-Electric Power in Ontario, 1890–1940" (Ph.D. thesis, University of Toronto, 1970), Chapter II; Christopher Armstrong, "The Mowat Heritage in Federal-Provincial Relations," in Swainson, *Oliver Mowat's Ontario*, 93–119, and Armstrong, "The Politics of Federalism: Ontario's Relations with the Federal Government, 1896–1941" (Ph.D. thesis, University of Toronto, 1972), Chapter 3.

reformist pressure result in legislation significantly different from the North American norm. In both those fields, however, sentiment for public ownership made greater progress than anywhere else on the continent. And it was fear of this which sent some businessmen scurrying to Ottawa for preventive measures before the fact or for compensation afterwards.

After 1905 the newly-elected Conservative government of James P. Whitney seized the opportunity presented by the silver rush at Cobalt to extract for public benefit a larger percentage of the profits of mineral exploitation. Mining claims were rigorously examined by inspectors and thrown open again if no mineralization could be shown. Some sections of the district were withheld from staking altogether and sold to the highest bidders. Several companies leased provincially controlled properties under the Cobalt townsite and the government railway. For a time the province even owned and operated its own silver mine! These *ad hoc* policies were favourably received by business groups in the southern part of the province, although they provoked a bitter reaction from the disappointed principals on the spot.

More controversially still, the new government eventually decided to build a publicly owned hydro-electric system to satisfy the rapidly growing energy requirements of the province. The application of hydro-electric technology to Niagara Falls in the last decade of the nineteenth century laid the foundations for rapid industrial development. Here at last was the energy base the province had lacked during the iron and coal phase of industrialism. To Ontario manufacturers the "white coal" of Niagara represented the hope of catching up, of release from a state of stagnation and comparative backwardness and dependence upon American coal. It was argued that such an important natural resource (still the property of the state) ought not to be left in the hands of monopolists, especially since their reputation as company promoters and traction magnates hardly inspired confidence. Adam Beck, a small manufacturer from London who became Minister responsible for power, forged these hopes and expectations into a public power movement intent upon the formation of a provincial monopoly for the generation and distribution of hydro-electricity to local, municipally owned utilities. This movement drew widespread support from the manufacturers, merchants, and municipal councillors of the burgeoning province, who recognized the growth-inducing potential of an abundant supply of power and illumination at cost.[6]

[6] Nelles, "Politics of Development," Chapters IV and V, discusses the regulation of the

The animosities which flowed naturally from vigorous government intervention in mining development and the fear instilled by the public power movement provided the material basis for another round of Dominion-provincial conflict. Besieged businessmen, surveying the hostile environment in which their companies had to work, went to Ottawa during this decade for three reasons. In the first instance, they sought to organize companies under federal charters with powers which they knew would not be granted by the provincial legislature. Secondly, some entrepreneurs, sensing the imminence of a crisis, hoped to persuade the central government to help avert the developing conflict through national regulation congenial to property. Finally, businessmen in extreme circumstances were reduced to begging the federal cabinet for disallowance to negate intolerable provincial acts. During this decade the Laurier administration thus came under pressure to assume the mantle already worn by the Supreme Court in the United States, that of guarantor of due process and defender of the sacred rights of private property.

The first method private interests used to entangle the federal government might be called "the charter ploy." The British North America Act gave the provinces power to incorporate only companies with "provincial objects." The federal parliament could charter concerns with national or international significance like banks or railways, as well as any undertaking whose works were declared to be "for the general advantage of Canada," whatever its scope. The development of industrial capitalism, however, blurred the distinction between "provincial objects" and "general advantage." A company with a plant in a single province could do business all over the country. Conversely, other businesses whose activities were limited to one province might be controlled in another jurisdiction. As a result, all that was required to justify a federal charter was a vague declaration of intent to do extra-provincial business or the claim that it was "for the general advantage of Canada."

Two groups of businessmen tried to capitalize on this legal confusion: those who sought rights through federal incorporation which would have been denied by the province, and those having already obtained privileges from the province who sought protection from further local regulation. In 1903, for example, William Mackenzie,

---

mining industry and the role of businessmen in the formation of the public power movement.

the great railroad and utilities promoter, petitioned for a federal charter for his Toronto & Hamilton Railway Company as a work for the general advantage of the Dominion. The railway was to have a perpetual franchise and the right of access into the city of Toronto without the payment of annual franchise fees. Such liberties would never have been granted by the Ontario legislature, where municipal influence was much stronger.[7]

In much the same manner, two consummate schemers, E. W. Backus and James Conmee, tried to take advantage of these federal powers of incorporation. Having extracted unusually generous concessions from the province to certain water powers on an international river, Backus hastily appealed to Ottawa in 1905 for a federal charter for his Ontario and Minnesota Power Company so that it would, he hoped, become impossible for the new Whitney administration to modify the agreement. He aimed to entrench his right to develop power on the Canadian side of the Rainy River and to export the bulk of it to his manufacturing concerns in the United States, putting this privilege beyond the influence of Adam Beck.[8]

The redoubtable James Conmee, M.P., bent his talents to an even more brazen coup a year later. He planned to organize a company to develop waterpower on the Nipigon River, but two obstacles stood in his way. First of all the provincial government owned a one chain reserve along both banks of the river, making it the riparian owner. Secondly, Adam Beck's Hydro-Electric Power Commission had already been established to regulate electrical production, and in certain instances to own and operate transmission lines. The Commission was most unlikely to approve Conmee's plans, much less his rate schedule. To evade provincial regulation, he tried to form a federally chartered company, ostensibly to develop power on the international Pigeon River. What he really wanted was the power of expropriation under the charter, which could then be used to seize the necessary provincial property on the Nipigon.[9]

[7] Canada, House of Commons, *Debates* [hereafter cited as *Debates*] July 7, 1903, 6116–17, 6092–93, 6198; August 3, 1903, 7813–14; August 21, 1903, 9420–28. Frederick Hamilton to J. S. Willison, August 12, 14, 15, 1903; Hamilton to A. H. U. Colquhoun, August 15, 1903; Willison Papers, Public Archives of Canada [hereafter PAC], 13140–52. H. H. Dewart to the Editor, Toronto *World*, July 10, 1903; Petition of the Municipal Representatives re the Principles of the Bill Incorporating the Toronto and Hamilton Railway Company, July 14, 1903; Fred Markey to Sir Wilfrid Laurier, July 15, 1903; *Memorandum Submitted in Support of the Toronto and Hamilton Railway Bill*, by H. H. Dewart July 22, 1903; Petition of W. D. Lighthall *et al.* to Sir Wilfrid Laurier and the Dominion Cabinet, July 27, 1903; Laurier Papers, PAC 75011, 75066–71, 75093–98, 76096–103, 76076–85.
[8] *Debates*, March 17, 24, 1905, 2720–25, 3135. R. W. Scott to James P. Whitney, March 30, 1905; Whitney to Scott, April 1, 1905; Whitney to Laurier, April 1, 1905; R. G. Code to Whitney, May 11, 1905; Whitney Papers, Provincial Archives of Ontario.
[9] *Debates*, February 15, 1909, 1026–53; April 19, 1909, 4520–38; May 3, 1909, 5373–5404; May 4, 1909, 5561; May 7, 1909, 5958–60; May 7, 1909. *Canadian Annual*

Taking the long view, a federal charter possessed other very important advantages. The tremendous profits earned by utility monopolies required the constant recapitalization of the firms. This could be done in the province, of course, but obtaining such permission from a legislature full of hostile municipal representatives could prove difficult and embarrassing, especially if profits above a certain percentage had to be shared with the local government. In Ottawa, far from such jealous scrutiny, utility magnates could reorganize their companies annually if necessary, liberally watering the stock each year. Even if earnings did not wholly warrant such increases, recapitalization might serve as a valuable deterrent to public ownership. When the inevitable occurred and the franchise either expired or was expropriated, the municipality could at least be made to pay dearly to recover its own property.[10]

For these reasons the 1890s and the first decade of the twentieth century witnessed a proliferation of federally incorporated utility companies whose activities were strictly local in scope. Lawyers and businessmen who counselled the move to Ottawa did so in the hope that inserting all contracts, agreements, and special powers into the act of incorporation would permit evasion of local obligations or deter expropriators. This was one way for capitalists with interests across the country to obtain federal protection from their municipal enemies.

The alarming growth of the movement for public ownership and control of hydro-electricity and mines in Ontario after 1905 convinced some business leaders that other defences were necessary. In order to save the rashest entrepreneurs from their own folly and to avoid vengeance being wreaked upon the rest, some businessmen came to believe that Ottawa should impose national regulation. They recognized that the uncompromising maintenance of a public-be-damned attitude in the face of evident public grievance, by the likes of William Mackenzie and the embattled directors of the Electrical Development Company of Toronto, merely fanned the flames of discontent. The radical drift of public opinion and the equally defiant barricade-building in some business quarters had to be arrested, even at the price of some loss of control over private property. They preferred toothless national regulation to avert the threat of serious local interference.

Review of Public Affairs, 1908, 283–84; 1909, 220–21. Conmee to Laurier, April 1, 1908; n.d. [April, 1909]; and replies, Laurier Papers, 138533–38, 155252–72. See also the correspondence between James P. Whitney and R. G. Code, March–May, 1909, in the Whitney Papers.

[10] This paragraph is based upon a reading of the E. H. Bronson and C. E. L. Porteous Papers, PAC. On the basis of these and other collections, we intend to make a further study of the franchise question in Ontario.

Canada's two foremost bankers, E. S. Clouston of the Bank of Montreal and B. E. Walker of the Bank of Commerce, for instance, were astounded at the rapid progress made by public power sentiment in Ontario. Walker, in particular, because his bank and his friends (like Mackenzie) had so much to lose from provincial interference, urged the federal government to intervene on behalf of capital. Walker thought the Cabinet should "take hold of the power situation throughout Canada and should give the people the same assurances of fair play that they have in the Railway Commission as applied to railways." [11] Adequate service would be guaranteed at reasonable rates, providing a "living profit" for investors. Regulation would be by specialists who shared business perceptions and recognized business problems, while the owners need no longer fear confiscation of their property.

Most persistent and influential in pressing this view on the Prime Minister was George Gibbons, the Canadian representative on the International Waterways Commission, who at that time was surveying the waterpower situation along the border. Gibbons knew the power industry intimately and had good connections with the financial elites of Montreal and Toronto. When the Laurier cabinet began to consider a bill to license electricity exports as a companion to a similar American law on imports, Gibbons urged the Prime Minister to seize this opportunity to lay down national standards of performance for the whole industry. The private power companies in Ontario had behaved badly, Gibbons admitted. Some had no intention of ever serving the domestic market, others would do so only at outrageous rates. The federal government, by controlling the right to export power, could coerce the companies into serving the local market better. Gibbons certainly hoped that this would have the additional advantage of pulling the rug from under Adam Beck and arresting "the socialistic progress" of Ontario.

A bill regulating exports, largely drafted by Gibbons, was eventually approved by the cabinet. Meanwhile, the public power movement had won a series of crucial battles for a government-owned transmission system. Partly as a consequence, the Electrical Development Company, largest of the private operators, was hovering on the brink of bankruptcy. In this desperate situation Gibbons reported to Laurier, "I have talked the matter over with the leading bankers in Toronto, and every one is favourable to the action of the Government, but in introducing it all are anxious that you should

[11] B. E. Walker to A. B. Aylesworth, January 11, 1907, Walker Papers, University of Toronto Archives. The Railway Commission had been created in 1903 to regulate rates and service of railroad companies under federal jurisdiction.

emphasize in the strongest way your intention to protect legitimate capital investment." Such a chance to give the lead in a vital area was unlikely to be repeated:

> A strong declaration that will give foreign capital encouragement to invest in Canada is very essential, and an equally strong declaration that corporations using the natural resources of the country for private gain must do so having due regard to the public interest.
>
> Excuse my urgency in this matter, but I do know public opinion is more alive to these interests than to any other, and that a strong declaration from you would be of great assistance to your friends.

On another occasion Gibbons reminded the Prime Minister of the political stature which Theodore Roosevelt had acquired from mediating the conflict between the trusts and the people. Irresponsible businessmen and public ownership demagogues alike in Canada needed to feel the big stick: "Through their stupidity a feeling is being created of hostility to capital, which is very likely to do great injury to the country." Abuses could best be prevented through federal regulation:

> It is not only politic but absolutely necessary for us, if the resources of our country are to be developed that the capitalists, whom we must call to our assistance to that end, should have positive assurance that when they invest their money in Canadian enterprises they have behind them as solid as the rock of Gibraltar the whole force of our Government as protection.
>
> It should be clearly announced that the dishonesty, which would lead to redemption of obligations or the anarchism which would destroy vested interests, should never have any footing on our soil.

Confrontation would permit the extremists to take charge, rather than "a conservative respector of property rights who yet can and will prevent corporate greed overlapping into extortion." The call for regulation coming from within the business community, then, was for protection from competition, in this case ruinous competition from a public agency.[12]

If some businessmen were urging the government to take on a new regulatory role, others were busy trying to bring their utilities' syndicates under the existing federal Board of Railway Commissioners, removing them from provincial control. J. M. Gibson,

[12] *Debates*, May 10, 1906, 3077–3101; May 29, 1906, 4035–77; January 29, 1907, 2229–80; March 19, 1907, 4946–64; *Statutes of Canada*, 6–7 Edw. VII, c. 16; Gibbons to Laurier, November 29, 1906; December 10, 1906, Strictly Private; January 7, 1907; January 22, 1907, Confidential; Laurier Papers, 116166–71, 116504–05, 117937–45, 118550–52. On the drive to avoid competition, see J. M. Bliss, " 'A Living Profit': Studies in the Social History of Canadian Business, 1883–1911," (Ph.D. Thesis, University of Toronto, 1972), Chapter 2.

former Attorney General of Ontario and a principal in the Hamilton electric and street railway companies, demonstrated special skill in this regard. The Ontario Railway and Municipal Board, unlike its federal counterpart, limited all municipal franchises to twenty-five years. Moreover, the federal board might prove more lenient in rate-fixing than the provincial commission. It took Gibson two full sessions of persistent lobbying amongst his political friends in Ottawa, but eventually he freed his interests from the thrall of the province and increased their capital to boot.[13]

Nevertheless, the federal cabinet had some reservations about the demands made upon it by businessmen. Traditionally the defender of provincial rights, the Liberals felt that national regulation ran against the grain except for matters specifically consigned to federal control by the constitution, such as banking. Other enterprises, as the Minister of Justice reminded the president of the Bank of Commerce in 1907, remained provincial responsibilities. However much aid and comfort the federal cabinet might wish to offer the injured parties, it could not summon up the courage to interfere.[14] Power exports, for instance, were licensed by Ottawa, but no more was done to regulate the industry. Despite this, the national financial community continued to look hopefully towards the federal authorities.

In direst necessity business interests resorted to a third method of attempting to nullify provincial enactments. If legislation could be shown to be unconstitutional or illegal, perhaps the federal cabinet might be induced to disallow the offending provincial acts. Although the Fisheries Reference had revealed the fullness of provincial powers, the nickel case supplied an encouraging example of what might be accomplished in the interests of property. What remained was to convince the federal government in each case that provincial regulations which violated vested rights constituted legitimate grounds for intervention, or rather, that the federal government should act to guarantee both substantive and procedural due process in the provinces.

Two sets of acts by the Ontario legislature raised particularly

[13] *Debates*, April 22, 1907, 7314–7407; April 23, 1907, 7485–91; April 26, 1907, 7915–17; February 24, 1908, 3721–30; February 25, 1908, 3703–04; March 3, 1908, 4368–70; March 6, 1908, 4543–44. *Canadian Annual Review of Public Affairs*, 1907, 494–96; 1908, 45. A. B. Aylesworth to James P. Whitney, February 18, 1907; Whitney to R. G. Code, January 21, 22, 1908, Private; Code to Whitney, February 7, 1908, enclosing, J. M. Gibson to Whitney, March 9, 22, 1907, and Whitney to Gibson, March 9, 1907; Whitney Papers. George P. Graham to Laurier, November 18, 1907, Confidential, Laurier Papers, 132283–84. Gibson to J. S. Willison, January 13, 1908, Private, Willison Papers, 11654–55.
[14] A. B. Aylesworth to B. E. Walker, January 18, 1907, Walker Papers.

anguished protests and resulted in urgent demands for disallowance. In the first case the province introduced legislation in 1906 reserving the mineral rights to the bed of Cobalt Lake, and in 1907 confirming its sale to the Cobalt Lake Mining Company for $1,085,000. A group of prospectors, intent upon a piece of sharp practice, insisted that they had staked the lakebed at a time when it was legally open for prospecting. The Florence Mining Company, to which they later transferred their rights, claimed to be the legitimate owner of the lakebed. Counsel for the company complained that the province had confiscated its property without compensation.

A second conflict arose over legislation confirming contracts between the Hydro-Electric Power Commission and its member municipalities. A standard contract had been approved by the ratepayers in the 1907 municipal elections. Subsequently certain changes were found to be necessary. Rather than returning the new contracts to the municipalities for a vote, the Commission simply secured the necessary remedial legislation from the province in 1909. This act forbade challenges to the contracts in the courts to prevent harassing suits by the hostile private power companies. Coming at the end of a long, bitter, and totally unsuccessful effort on the part of utilities promoters to defeat the public power movement, this naturally inspired the fiercest resentment. Since the Ontario Hydro-Electric Power Commission ultimately rested upon these contracts, they determined to fight to the last ditch against this massive interference with the rights of property.[15]

With the Cobalt Lake and Hydro legislation, Ontario seemed to have gone too far. The constitution might grant the province jurisdiction over property and civil rights, but could it use this power to violate vested interests, then deny them access to the courts? To admit this placed all such rights in peril. E. R. Wood of Dominion Securities Corporation argued that "the right of Federal veto was incorporated in our Constitution as a safeguard for private property, and it may serve at the same time to save the credit of the Dominion in the financial centre of the world."[16]

When the federal cabinet heard the arguments against the Cobalt Lake legislation in 1908, however, it reluctantly ruled on behalf of the province. The Minister of Justice found that this legislation regarding the management of the Crown lands fell within Ontario's

[15] For details of the Cobalt Lake and Hydro controversies, see Nelles, "Politics of Development," 299–308, 466–474.
[16] E. R. Wood to Laurier, June 17, 1909, Personal, Laurier Papers, 157057–60. This attempt to use the power of disallowance to protect property rights has obvious parallels to the use of the 14th Amendment in the United States.

jurisdiction. The Florence Mining Company appealed to the courts, but Mr. Justice W. R. Riddell in dismissing the case remarked:

> The Legislature within its jurisdiction can do anything which is not naturally impossible and is restrained by no rule, human or divine. If it be that the plaintiffs acquired any rights — which I am far from finding — the Legislature has the power to take them away. The prohibition "Thou shalt not steal," has no legal force upon a sovereign body, and there would be no necessity for compensation to be given.

Riddell's statement, the logical extension of the Privy Council's judgment in the Fisheries Reference, confirmed that in the event of such abuses the defence must be political rather than legal. This forthright decision, Premier Whitney gleefully confided to his brother, ought to "settle the pirates for a while."

It did not; the Florence Mining Company carried its appeal as far as the Privy Council, to no avail. These adverse judgments by the political and legal authorities virtually settled in advance the outcome of the appeal against the Hydro legislation. Once again Mr. Justice Riddell upheld the right of the province to remove its legislation from challenge in the courts: "I have not to tell the Legislature what to do; I am a creature of the Legislature — though not a subservient creature. If the Legislature says, it is not your duty to try such and such action, it is my duty not to try it. I am here to carry out the laws." In another case, Mr. Justice Falconbridge concurred: [17]

> We have heard a good deal recently about the jurisdiction of the Province, a good deal of complaint about the exercise of its powers; but there is no doubt that the highest authority has declared that within its own jurisdiction it is supreme; in fact, while it seems rather severe I suppose that there is not any doubt that if the Legislature had chosen to confiscate — the word that is used — the farm of the plaintiff without any compensation, they would have had a perfect right to do it in law, if not in morals.

Businessmen hostile to the Hydro legislation thus had to rely upon the discretionary power of disallowance. Counsel for the power companies argued that the provincial act violated common law notions of vested rights. Though technically constitutional, the act trespassed upon what would be called due process in the United States. F. H. Crysler went so far as to argue that provincial legisla-

---

[17] The provincial government triumphantly printed 1,000 copies of the Appeal Court's decision in the Cobalt Lake case as a pamphlet, *The Florence Mining Company v. The Cobalt Lake Mining Company: Ontario Court of Appeal* (Toronto, 1909). See also J. P. Whitney to E. C. Whitney, April 7, 1909, Whitney Papers. *Canadian Annual Review of Public Affairs*, 1908, 285–87, 1909, 381–83.

tion could be "unconstitutional without being prohibited in the British North America Act" when it contradicted its "spirit and purport." Questioned by the cabinet, he admitted that he was using the word "unconstitutional" in a political sense, the legislation in question being unjust rather than *ultra vires*. Since the courts were powerless to act, Crysler claimed that the federal ministry had a duty to step in and protect private rights and natural justice. The companies supported this contention with a pamphlet containing the assorted grumblings of constitutional authorities and the financial press, but again the federal authorities declined to act. The Minister of Justice restated his belief that an appeal against the abuse of provincial power lay not to him but to the local electorate.

Laurier and leading members of his cabinet took few pains to conceal their sympathies with injured entrepreneurs despite their refusal to intervene. In numerous consoling letters, the Prime Minister and Minister of Justice admitted that an injustice had occurred but regretted that their hands were tied. A. B. Aylesworth told the House of Commons on March 1, 1909, that the Cobalt Lake legislation had confiscated property. He upheld Ontario's right to do so or even to repeal Magna Carta if it chose, although he made his displeasure at this state of affairs equally clear. Had the same act been passed before 1896, he said, it would certainly have been disallowed in order to protect vested rights from provincial interference.[18]

Despite this sympathy, Ontario businessmen who tried to use these three strategies — federal incorporation, regulation, and disallowance — generally failed. Those connected with the capital market were convinced that their interests would be served best by a powerful central government. They found ranged against them local business groups who recognized that their goals of cheap power, strict regulation of other utilities, and greater revenue from resource exploitation (thereby making direct taxation unnecessary) were most readily attainable through the exercise of provincial authority in a decentralized federation. So long as someone else's ox was being gored, this latter group had little hesitation in working to impose restrictions on the rights of property.

Every effort to escape provincial control produced its reaction.

[18] *Debates*, March 1, 1909, 1750–58. Letters to Laurier protesting the confiscatory Ontario acts during the summer and fall of 1909 from such financial luminaries as B. E. Walker, E. R. Wood, John Blaikie, F. A. Vanderlip, C. W. Kerr, and James Mason may be found in the Laurier Papers. For details of the struggle over disallowance, see Armstrong, "Politics of Federalism," Chapter 4.

Those who succeeded in getting federal charters soon found the advantage nullified by Ontario. Each use of the charter ploy simply heightened provincial vigilance about the proceedings in the Private Bills Committee of the House of Commons. Forceful argument and an occasional mild threat eventually compelled the federal government to require its companies to obey provincial regulation, which took most of the sport out of the Dominion-provincial game. Ontario's militancy ensured that the federal system would not become a means of escape from local regulation. Similarly, the drift of constitutional interpretation and the progress of the public power movement in Ontario cut the ground from under those who believed that Ottawa should have expanded powers to regulate business and should use the power of disallowance in defense of vested rights.

The effort by local business and manufacturing interests to induce the province to play an active regulatory role in the mining and utilities sectors brought them into collision with the representatives of capital.[19] The outcome of this struggle made clear the fullness of arbitrary state authority vis à vis property and vested rights, which severely shook the pillars of Canadian finance. Sympathy from Ottawa was no substitute for protection, and many of them must have hoped that some action would be taken to protect the rights of property in future.

Efforts to Amend the Constitution

The immediate consequence of this was an effort to amend the constitution in the interests of capital. Goldwin Smith declared melodramatically from his deathbed that the provincial government had "opened the doors of confiscation & closed the doors of justice." Governor General Earl Grey, himself closely linked to British financial interests, cast about for an Alexander Hamilton to stem the anticipated tide of repudiated obligations.[20] American

[19] In this pattern of conflict there were, of course, anomalies. In 1900 J. M. Gibson and the other members of the Hamilton syndicate had to rely on the province for the manufacturing condition on nickel; in 1907 Gibson turned to Ottawa for protection of his utilities empire. To add to the confusion, he had, as Attorney General in 1903, strongly protested to Ottawa about the use of the charter ploy by local electric railways in Ontario. But by 1907 he himself had become a utilities magnate, and as we have seen, quickly set about protecting his interests from interference by Ontario through federal regulation. In the same way Henry M. Pellatt may be found on different sides at different times. As the promoter of the Cobalt Lake Mining Company he applauded the outcome of the great battle for provincial rights fought on his behalf. Yet that very victory meant that as vice-president of the tottering Toronto utilities syndicate he would lose the war in 1910.

[20] Lord Grey to Laurier, April 10, 1910, Laurier Papers, April 10, 1910, 206676-94, reports Smith's deathbed conversation. Lord Grey himself had a deep interest in various Canadian companies, and his son-in-law Arthur Grenfell, was a London banker with wide Canadian interests.

models, in fact, were much on the minds of the Canadian financial community, well aware of the broader legal protection enjoyed by property owners in the United States. While the fate of the Hydro legislation was still being debated, a well known corporation lawyer wrote to the Prime Minister to suggest that, since disallowance now appeared to be a political impossibility, the constitution urgently needed revision. If the B.N.A. Act were amended to protect the rights of contract as the American constitution did, "demagogism" could no longer run rampant. Laurier's reply demonstrated his customary sympathy for the propertied, tempered as always by political canniness: [21]

> I have indeed often thought that it would be well to introduce such an amendment to our constitution. The provision of the American constitution protecting the sacredness of contract has been a source of incalculable strength to the Union. I have always regretted that such a provision had not been thought of by the Fathers of our own Confederation. To, however, undo such an omission is a work which would require some serious consideration before we could plunge into it.

However loudly they might complain in private about the perfidy of the Ontario government, most members of the national financial elite were reluctant to engage in public controversy. So intimately were business and politics linked, so diverse were the interests of a Henry Pellatt, a Byron Walker, or a William Mackenzie, that they saw it would be imprudent to antagonize the Whitney administration further. Thus it fell to that tireless busybody Lord Grey, not similarly constrained, to take up the campaign for an amendment to the constitution to make Canada a land fit for investors to live in.

Near the end of 1910 he wrote to a number of political and business leaders to urge action. Sir James Whitney replied firmly that the threat posed to private property by his government had been grossly exaggerated by his opponents. He was, he declared, "a straight-out champion . . . of the rights of property and of vested rights." [22] Moreover, he could see no prospect of the provincial electorate approving such an amendment: "It would simply be asking them to hand back a part of the jurisdiction given them by

[21] Wallace Nesbitt to Laurier, November 1, 1909; Laurier to Nesbitt, November 3, 1909; Laurier Papers, 161564–67.
[22] Whitney to Grey, December 14, 1910, Whitney Papers. Whitney spoke the truth. Before becoming Premier, he and his brother had been involved with some of these same men in a railway promotion. See Whitney to E. C. Whitney, February 7, 8, 16, March 9, April 1, 1899, Letter Book, 1899, Whitney Papers. Though not himself a member of the financial elite, he clearly shared their outlook. He was a late and reluctant convert to public ownership, who became convinced of its necessity only by the stubbornness and violence of the reaction of the private power interests.

the British North America Act — and for the reason that they, the people of the Provinces, cannot be trusted with the exercise of such power! No other reason could be given — at least I can think of no other." [23]

Despite his suffering at Ontario's hands, Byron Walker explained frankly why he and his kind could not become involved in such an agitation:

> I do not know of any prominent person who would publicly avow the necessity of an amendment to the British North America Act because of such Provincial legislation, although there are very many who think such an amendment necessary. Men like Mackenzie have too many dealings with the Government to be willing to act, although they are precisely the ones who are interested in the status of Canadian securities abroad.

He could only suggest to the Governor General that American investors might be inspired to raise the matter with the federal government. No more was heard of the plan.[24]

It would have been ironic indeed if Canadians had been persuaded to incorporate into their constitution safeguards for the rights of property on the American model. As early as 1905 Justice Oliver Wendell Holmes had pointed out in his classic dissent in *Lochner v. New York* that,

> It is settled by various opinions of this court that state constitutions and state laws may regulate life in ways that we as legislators might think as injudicious, or if you like as tyrannical, as this, and which equally with this interfere with the liberty of contract. . . . The 14th Amendment does not enact Mr. Herbert Spencer's Social Statics. . . . A constitution is not intended to embody a particular economic theory, whether of paternalism and the organic relation of the citizen to the state or of *laisser-faire*.

Thereafter the trend of judicial interpretation was gradually reversed, and due process confined to a somewhat narrower sphere.[25]

CONCLUSION

The institutional framework within which these conflicts took place was different from that in the United States in important ways. Provincial ownership of lands and natural resources provided Ontario with a means of directing and regulating economic development not available to the states. Moreover, Ontario did not labor under any constitutional limitation upon the spending of public funds for internal improvements, as did a state like Wisconsin.[26]

[23] Whitney to Grey, January 9, 1911, Private, Whitney Papers.
[24] Walker to Grey, January 30, 1911, Private, Walker Papers.
[25] Quoted in Kelly and Harbison, *The American Constitution*, 525, 685–721.
[26] See James Willard Hurst, *Law and Economic Growth: The Legal History of the*

Because of the province's particular economic situation and the decentralized nature of the federal system, provincial Progressives in Ontario were able to create a publicly owned hydro-electric system unique in North America.

Canada's federal system closed the normal route of escape from the local to the national level of government, where reform impulses could usually be redirected by big business. This created a substantially different legal climate for enterprise in Canada than in the United States. The combination of local control and parliamentary sovereignty allowed Ontario Progressives to overcome the usual legal obstacles to interference with the sacred rights of private property. Confined to a battleground at the local level, in a state untrammelled by due process and with unlimited power within its fields of jurisdiction, the financial community found themselves at a distinct disadvantage. In Canada it would not be the case that "national progressivism was able to short-circuit state progressivism, to hold nascent radicalism in check by feeding the illusions of its leaders . . . ."[27]

The financiers responsible for the protection of massive amounts of capital imported into Canada insisted that this local insurgency, if left unchecked, would lead to a wholesale flight of capital. Their great worry was that the success of one public ownership experiment might lead to the extension of the principle. Local business Progressives, who supported the intervention of the province into these fields, could easily laugh off the accusation that they were dangerous radicals. They were only trying to make the existing system work, and they were simply better served by public ownership of certain utilities and strict regulation of others. Behind the collision of the two levels of government were competing economic interests, clothed in the raiment of principle whenever possible.

Local control in Ontario did permit one new form of business enterprise to appear. This was, however, never generalized into a radical critique of industrial capitalism. The fears of the financial community that the principle of public ownership would be expanded beyond the boundaries of the utilities and mines proved chimerical. The reason why that was so, of course, is another and much longer story.

Lumber Industry in Wisconsin, 1836–1915 (Cambridge, Mass., 1964), for a discussion of the institutional setting of business enterprise in Wisconsin; see also Harry N. Scheiber, "Government and the Economy: Studies in the 'Commonwealth' Policy in Nineteenth Century America," *Journal of Interdisciplinary History*, III (1972), 135–151.

[27] Kolko, *Triumph of Conservatism*, 285.

By Michael Bliss
ASSISTANT PROFESSOR OF HISTORY
UNIVERSITY OF TORONTO

Another Anti-Trust Tradition: Canadian Anti-Combines Policy, 1889-1910

❡ *Professor Bliss suggests that the Canadian anti-trust tradition was much more similar to the British experience than to the policies adopted in the United States. At no time, he argues, did Canadian legislation significantly expand the common law prohibition of undue or unreasonable restraints of trade, and the few prosecutions after 1900 had no significant effect in inhibiting the thrust of business resistance to market forces.*

Canada's first statute relating to the general problem of preserving economic competition was passed in 1889, one year before the American Sherman Anti-trust Act. In the next twenty years the legislation was amended, and there were experiments with other anti-combines devices, culminating in an attempt to provide investigative procedures in the Combines Investigation Act of 1910. This legislative record has led scholars to couple Canada with the United States as the two nations which in the late nineteenth and early twentieth centuries tried to arrest economic consolidation by legislating in favour of competition.[1] American historians have long debated the extent and effectiveness of the American anti-trust commitment from 1890 through the Wilson administrations, weighing substantial anti-trust rhetoric against erratic and perhaps ineffectual administration of the legislation.[2] The Canadian case is somewhat more clear: Canadian anti-combines legislation during these years was insignificant and ineffectual; it did not reflect a serious desire by legislators to resist economic consolidation or restore the forces of the free market.

There had been sporadic complaints about "rings" and "trusts" operating in Canada since at least the early 1870s, but the "com-

Business History Review, Vol. XLVII, No. 2 (Summer, 1973). Copyright © The President and Fellows of Harvard College.

[1] W. Friedmann, *Law in a Changing Society* (Berkeley, Cal., 1959), 281–87; Friedmann, ed., *Anti-Trust Laws: A Comparative Symposium* (Toronto, 1956).

[2] Hans B. Thorelli, *The Federal Antitrust Policy* (London, 1954); William Letwin, *Law and Economic Policy in America* (Edinburgh, 1967).

bines question" as such did not become a matter of government concern until February 1888, when a Select Committee of the House of Commons was appointed "to examine into and report upon the nature, extent and effect of certain combinations said to exist with reference to the purchase and sale, or manufacture and sale, in Canada, of any foreign or Canadian products." [3] These combinations were being criticized in the press and by N. Clarke Wallace, a Conservative Member of Parliament who had raised the issue as a consumer's friend in the 1887 Toronto mayoralty election (claiming that the "purity and good government" candidate was a member of the local coal ring) and again in the House of Commons in 1888 as the champion of merchants discriminated against by a grocers' combine. Wallace was appointed chairman of the Select Committee. In two months of sittings it heard sixty-three witnesses and reported that while "the evils produced by combinations . . . have not by any means been fully developed as yet in this country, . . . sufficient evidence of their injurious tendencies and effects is given to justify legislative action for suppressing the evils arising from these and similar combinations and monopolies." [4] Wallace immediately introduced a bill, copied from legislation pending in New York State, to prohibit combines that discriminated against third parties, restricted competition, "unreasonably" enhanced prices, or "unduly" restrained trade.

The British common law covering conspiracies in restraint of trade had been significantly relaxed in the nineteenth century and by the 1880s gave businessmen wide leeway for restrictive agreements. In the leading Canadian case before 1888, the terms of a price-fixing salt combine had been held in 1871 to be an acceptable restraint of trade because of the British abolition in 1844 of the offenses of engrossing, forestalling, and regrating. Its members were permitted to bring the force of law against another member who had tried to break the agreement.[5] Some Parliamentarians were aware that common law no longer offered much recourse to those who wanted to prevent such restrictions as price-fixing or limitation of production; others only knew that the law was abstruse and difficult

[3] House of Commons, *Debates*, February 29, 1888, 28–35.

[4] "Report of the Select Committee to Investigate and Report Upon Alleged Combinations in Manufactures, Trade and Insurance in Canada," House of Commons, *Journals*, 1888, Appendix 3, 10.

[5] John A. Ball, Jr., *Canadian Anti-Trust Legislation* (Baltimore, 1934), 21–22. Other standard sources on the development of Canadian anti-combines policy are Lloyd G. Reynolds, *The Control of Competition in Canada* (Cambridge, Mass., 1940); Vincent W. Bladen, *An Introduction to Political Economy* (Toronto, rev. ed., 1956), ch. VIII; and L. A. Skeoch, ed., *Restrictive Trade Practices in Canada* (Toronto, 1966).

to enforce. New legislation was necessary if the combinations un-covered by Wallace's committee were to be suppressed.

Nevertheless, when Wallace's anti-combines bill emerged from the legislative process in the spring of 1889, it had become only "An Act to Declare the Common Law," making it a misdemeanour to conspire, combine, agree, or arrange, "unlawfully:" [6]

(a) To unduly limit the facilities for transporting, producing, manu-facturing, supplying, storing or dealing in any article or commodity which may be a subject of trade or commerce; or —
(b) To restrain or injure trade or commerce in relation to any such article or commodity; or —
(c) To unduly prevent, limit, or lessen the manufacture or production of any such article or commodity, or to unreasonably enhance the price thereof; or —
(d) To unduly prevent or lessen competition in the production, manu-facture, purchase, barter, sale, transportation or supply of any such article or commodity, or in the price of insurance upon person or property.

At best the act was declaratory legislation, pointing out that the common law, which had never been out of effect, was in effect. It not only did nothing to strengthen the by then very weak common law restrictions on restraints of trade, but it prescribed less severe penalties for conspiracy in restraint of trade than the parallel sections of the Criminal Code, and by its phraseology of offences it may have shifted the onus of proving reasonableness from the defence to the prosecution.[7] The tortuous use of "unlawfully," "unduly," and "un-reasonably" even opened Parliament to ridicule for having declared that a combination could now unlawfully advance prices if it did not do so unduly, or vice-versa. One member of the Liberal Opposi-tion summed up most people's feelings about the legislation when he remarked, "It need not be opposed; it will die from sheer inani-tion." [8]

The basic reasons for this less than half-hearted legislative re-sponse to the recommendations of the Select Committee of 1888 stemmed from the kinds of combination uncovered in that investi-gation and the arguments made in their defence. Despite the com-mittee's conclusion that new legislation was needed, it had not in fact uncovered a particularly alarming situation. With one in-significant exception, the combines investigated were loosely-knit trade associations — small distributors or producers of groceries, watch-cases, binder-twine, coal, oatmeal, stoves, agricultural imple-

[6] Canada, *Statutes*, 1889, 52 Vic., ch. 41.
[7] Reynolds, *Control of Competition*, 131–32; House of Commons, *Debates*, July 20, 1891, 2579.
[8] House of Commons, *Debates*, April 30, 1889, 1690.

ments, and undertakers' supplies who were attempting with widely varying degrees of success to fix prices and/or limit production and entry. The most iniquitous combine was the Coal Section of the Toronto Board of Trade, whose members fixed prices, engaged in collusive bidding, and tightly enforced their arrangements. Elias Rogers, Toronto's most prominent coal merchant and the recent clean government candidate for mayor, was humiliated before the committee; the organization was subsequently expelled from the Board of Trade. Most attention, however, focused on the Dominion Wholesale Grocers' Guild, a national organization operating price-fixing agreements with manufacturers of tobacco, starch, baking powder, pickles, sugar, and other articles. The sugar combine was the most important and controversial of its arrangements: the Guild had agreed with the sugar refineries that sales of white sugar would be made to Guild members on more favourable terms than to non-members, membership being conditional on adhering to its fixed prices and doing no retailing. The chief witnesses against the Guild were two non-member wholesalers unable to get sugar at Guild prices.[9]

Although the Wholesale Grocers' Guild was condemned as "obnoxious to the public interest" by Wallace's Committee,[10] it had by no means the worst of the debate about its activities and the principle of businessmen combining to limit competition. Guildsmen based their defense on the "demoralization" of the grocery trade before the combine's formation, a state of cut-throat competition particularly evident and harmful in the universal use of sugar as a loss leader. How could he be classed as an oppressor of the public, wrote a wholesale grocer in 1888, when all he was trying to do by joining the Guild was "struggling for the reasonable right of making a small profit on what I sell?" What was unreasonable about aiming to make a "living profit" on sugar?[11] The Guild maintained that under the combine, its sugar profits ranged between 2.75 and 4.52 per cent on costs, whereas the average accepted rate of return on wholesale groceries was 4.50 per cent. A $1,000 cheque was offered to the mayor of Toronto to be distributed to city charities if these figures were successfully disputed. They were not.[12] Further, Guild officials successfully discredited the chief hostile witness at the investigation by showing that he had been one of the charter

[9] "Report of the Select Committee," *passim.*
[10] *Ibid.,* 5.
[11] *Monetary Times,* May 25, 1888, 1448.
[12] Hugh Blain, *Combines: An Address Delivered Before the Board of Trade of the City of Toronto* (Toronto, 1889).

members of the organization in 1884, had taken the lead in originating the combines on tobacco, baking powder, and starch, and had been among the first to suggest fixing a price on sugar. He had never disapproved of the Guild on principle, and he was forced to admit that he was still in favour of all but the sugar combine.[13] Fears that the Guild was engaged in private law-making were countered with the argument that a majority of the trade had approved of these reasonable safeguards against excessive and dangerous commercial liberty.[14]

More generally, the late 1880s and early 1890s were a time of near-universal criticism of unregulated competition in the Canadian business community. Businessmen large and small were insisting that trade restrictions were absolutely necessary if business was to produce a "living profit." Combination was seen as a reasonable act of self-protection, exactly parallel to the restrictionism practised by professional bodies and trade unions. It was claimed that combinations could only fix prices at reasonable levels because of the pressures of public opinion in an age when agreements were publicized and for fear of inducing competition and disintegration. In a scathing denunciation of attempts to legislate against combines, the Council of the Toronto Board of Trade argued that "capital, like everything else, has, by universal consent, an undoubted right to protection when in danger, and to refuse it would be oppression in its worst form." "Righteous combinations," the Board felt, were "a benefit to all concerned." [15] Business lobbyists descended on Ottawa to ensure that anti-combines legislation did not adversely affect their interests, and there was no corresponding lobby of "free enterprise" businessmen interested in breaking combines.

W. J. Ashley, the country's leading economist, felt that the case against the Guild was not proven, that its activities forced a re-examination of the classical economists' approval of competition, and he stressed "the worry and laceration of spirit, and the vulgarization of business" involved in unregulated competition.[16] The one liberal intellectual journal in Canada moved from instinctive opposition to all combines in 1888 to the realization a year later that they were probably a necessary defence against competition and should be

[13] "Report of the Select Committee," 88–89, 113, 23.
[14] Blain, *Combines; Monetary Times*, April 5, 1889, 1158.
[15] Public Archives of Canada, John A. Macdonald Papers, p. 150845, "Report of Committee on Combines to the Council of the Board of Trade of the City of Toronto," February 26, 1889; for details of resistance to competition see my unpublished doctoral thesis, "A Living Profit: Studies in the Social History of Canadian Business, 1883–1911" (University of Toronto, 1972), chs. 1–3.
[16] "The Canadian Sugar Combine," *University Quarterly Review*, I, 1 (February 1890), 12–39.

regulated by government rather than outlawed.[17] It was generally felt by businessmen and legislators that there could be extortionate combinations and monopolies, and that these were a severe problem in the United States (plagued by "Alps upon Alps of combines," one MP claimed),[18] but that the few instances of these in Canada could be dealt with if the common law were made known.

The only legislators who wanted to swim against the current of business opinion on the competition question were members of the Liberal Opposition, who were particularly concerned about the high cost of consumer goods. But they, too, were relatively unconcerned about specific anti-combines legislation because of their conviction that combines were the natural consequence of a far greater evil, the Conservatives' National Policy of tariff protection. Tariff reduction was the Liberal panacea for all problems of combination and monopoly, and they had no interest in cooperating with protectionist Conservatives like Wallace in what appeared to be a political ploy to dodge the real issue.

In truth the passing of the anti-combines act of 1889 was no more than a political sham, the central figure in which was Canada's self-proclaimed trust-buster, N. Clarke Wallace. He deliberately watered down his own bill until it was ineffectual. In April 1889 he withdrew the original bill, explaining that objections had been made to the possibility of a new offence being created, "and the judges might perhaps interpret the Bill more severely than was intended," and replaced it with a new bill — the one containing the word "unlawfully" — which he explained was only intended to declare the English common law.[19] He agreed that his bill would not prohibit cotton manufacturers from combining to limit production, and in later hearings he only singled out one particularly obnoxious salt combine, which his committee had not investigated, as an object of his legislation.[20] He did object when the Senate re-inserted the various "unduly"s and the "unreasonably" in amendments to his bill (as further protection against the creation of new offences), but he felt the legislation would nonetheless "be a terror to evil doers, and it will show that the Parliament of Canada have put on record their condemnation of the illegal practices we have been legislating against." This was fraudulent political posturing, designed partly to continue to enhance Wallace's popular reputation as the enemy of combines, almost certainly also as part of a calculated Conservative

[17] *The Week*, March 29, April 19, May 3, 1888.
[18] House of Commons, *Debates*, April 22, 1889, 1441.
[19] *Ibid.*, April 8, 1889, 1113.
[20] Toronto *Globe*, April 13, 17, 1889.

manoeuvre to deflect criticism from the combine-creating effects of the protective tariff.[21]

As expected, the legislation languished in desuetude. In 1890 and 1891 Wallace tried to squeeze more political mileage out of the issue by proposing amendments which he claimed would strengthen the Act. But they would only have removed "unduly" and "unreasonably" from the statute; it was well understood that the word "unlawfully" made it ineffectual, and Wallace did not propose to change this.[22] No combine was broken up by the anti-combine act of 1889; the one prosecution resulted in acquittal because no common law offence could be proven.[23]

In 1897 Wilfrid Laurier's government implemented the approach to combines policy that Liberals had advocated in 1888: a clause in the new tariff permitted the Governor-in-Council to remove the tariff on any commodity found to be controlled by a combine to the detriment of the consumer.[24] Anti-combine policy in this form was little more effective than the old Wallace Act.[25] Laurier's Minister of Finance later admitted that in initiating the policy he had not understood either the damage tariff reductions might do to non-combining producers or that the most serious combinations were among retailers who could not be reached by tariff juggling.[26] In any case, having swapped their free trade principles for the prospect of power in 1896, the Liberal Party as a whole was no longer very inclined to challenge either the tariff system or the embarrassing combines that might be found nesting under its wing.

The 1889 Wallace Act (incorporated into the Criminal Code in the general recodification of 1892) suddenly became enforceable in 1900 when Parliament deleted the crucial qualifying word "unlawfully," thus creating new law. Incredible as it seems, this happened by accident when a Senator who prided himself on his drafting ability suggested omitting the word in order to get rid of the "sur-

[21] This account and interpretation of the passing of the legislation differs from those of Ball and Reynolds, who, by failing to notice that Wallace himself watered down his bill, credit him with good intentions and blame the final product on business lobbyists. There is also controversy about another section of the act affecting trade unions' exemption from the legislation. Liberals claimed, and some historians have agreed, that the Act did remove unions' exemption from prosecution for conspiracy in restraint of trade. This was not the case. For a more detailed account of the legislative history of the bill, see Bliss, "A Living Profit," 94–106.

[22] House of Commons, *Debates*, July 20, 1891, 2560.

[23] Reynolds, *Control of Competition in Canada*, 135.

[24] O. J. McDiarmid, *Commercial Policy in the Canadian Economy* (Cambridge, Mass., 1946), 207; Ball, *Canadian Anti-Trust Legislation*, 13–15.

[25] Ball, *Canadian Anti-Trust Legislation*, 14–17. The only action taken was an investigation of a combine among Canadian paper manufacturers in 1902. This eventually led to a 40 per cent reduction in the tariff on newsprint, but there was, significantly, no criminal prosecution of a combination exposed as unduly raising prices.

[26] House of Commons, *Debates*, April 27, 1910, 7991; *Toronto Star*, February 27, 1909.

plusage" in the section, wording which "as a matter of art, ought not to prevail." He was not practising duplicity, for a few weeks later he explicitly defended the right of combination and the need to keep "unduly" and "unreasonably" in the law.[27] None in Parliament realized what the amendment implied, and the change in the law went totally unnoticed in business circles until 1903, when the first of several actions was launched against price-fixing trade associations.[28] Even then only certain sections of the business community were alarmed by the situation. In 1908 the Retail Merchants' Association of Canada began a campaign to have the Criminal Code re-amended, but was refused support from the Canadian Manufacturers' Association on the ground that "any agitation . . . may only serve to stir things up and direct attention to a law that officials are lax in enforcing." [29]

By 1910 the Laurier government was under considerable public pressure to take further action against combines. Serious inflation was being blamed on the continuance of price-fixing combines in distribution and on a major consolidation movement that had broken out in 1909 and was creating a roster of giant Canadian corporations — Amalgamated Asbestos, National Breweries, Canada Cement, Carriage Factories Ltd., etc. — suspiciously similar to American trusts.[30] Provincial attorneys-general (constitutionally responsible for administration of the Criminal Code) were erratic in their enforcement of the existing legislation because of the difficulty and expense of investigation to gather evidence against combinations. Responding to these concerns, Laurier's Minister of Labour, William Lyon Mackenzie King, brought in new legislation which became the Combines Investigation Act of 1910. But the Act only set up machinery to determine whether or not combinations existed that were unduly or unreasonably in restraint of trade.[31] It did not alter the definition of illegal combinations, leaving Canadian businessmen free to enter into their "due" and "reasonable" restraints of trade.

[27] Senate, *Debates*, June 26, 1899, 492–94; July 17, 1899, 781. A year later the 1899 draft amendments passed both Houses without comment.
[28] Ball, *Canadian Anti-Trust Legislation*, 24–34. Action was taken against Ontario coal dealers in 1903, drug manufacturers in 1904, master plumbers in Ontario in 1905, the Dominion Wholesale Grocers' Guild in 1906, and lumber dealers on the prairies in 1907. Only the Guild was acquitted. For judicial interpretation of the legislation, see Skeoch, ed., *Restrictive Trade Practices in Canada*, 31–89.
[29] Canadian Manufacturers' Association, Archives, Executive Council, *Minutes*, January 16, 1908.
[30] *Canadian Annual Review, 1909*, 188–89, 255–260.
[31] Upon the application of any six persons a judge could, after a hearing, order the Minister of Labour to appoint an investigating commission to determine if a combine existed in violation of the Criminal Code. Reports were to be made public and penalties were provided for continuing the offence.

The Combines Investigation Act was drafted and defended in full consciousness of the American debate on the problems of industrial consolidation. Mackenzie King proved himself a thorough-going Canadian "New Nationalist" on the trust question, quoting Jeremiah Jenks, William E. Collier, Theodore Roosevelt, and others on the necessity for distinguishing between good and bad trusts, and spelling out the government's determination to avoid the mistakes Americans had made with what King thought was the unenforceable and anachronistic Sherman Act. Taking great pain to deny the popular belief in a connection between the cost of living and the merger movement, King fully accepted the argument that most mergers promoted economic efficiency. He instanced the promises of efficiency made in the prospectus of the Canada Cement Company as one of the "obvious examples" of how mergers could benefit the country. At the time this cement monopoly (the culmination of the later Lord Beaverbrook's Canadian career) was rightly the prime target of Canadian anti-trust agitation. On the other hand King found harmful combinations so little in evidence that he had to refer members to the 1888 investigation for examples of unreasonable combines. Business journals were correct in perceiving that King's legislation would reduce public criticism of mergers without doing any serious damage to corporate interests. This was his explicit intention.[32] The Act was invoked only once, against an American shoe machine monopoly with inconclusive results, before it was repealed in 1919.[33]

Neither in the 1889 nor in the 1910 legislation had the Canadian government conceded anything substantial to defenders of a competitive economy; only the absent-minded amendment of 1900 opened a loophole for the courts to begin to enforce new law. But at no time did Canadian legislation significantly expand the common law prohibition of undue or unreasonable restraints of trade, and the handful of prosecutions after 1900 had no significant effect in inhibiting the thrust of business resistance to market forces. In 1910, twenty-two years after its methods had first been exposed, the Dominion Wholesale Grocers' Guild was still recording its price-fixing arrangements in its minute books, the secretary of the Retail Merchants' Association was urging retailers to "not be ashamed to say that they were holding meetings to fix prices," and

[32] House of Commons, *Debates*, April 12, 1910, 6802–6861; PAC, W. L. M. King Papers, vol C3, File 25.
[33] *Monetary Times*, November 26, 1910, 2213; Ball, *Canadian Anti-Trust Legislation*, 45–59.

large sectors of Canadian manufacturing had fallen under monopolistic or oligopolistic control because of the merger movement.[34]

Some of the reasons for the lack of a strong Canadian competition policy are clear from the preceding accounts of the legislation. The 1889 act was passed in a period when the dominant form of combination was the loosely-knit trade association, usually composed of small businessmen, struggling without much prospect of success to stabilize markets and profit margins in a period of fierce competition. The defense of these practices was persuasive enough that Canadian legislators were very careful not to enact anything like a blanket condemnation of restraints of trade, much more careful than the American Congress would be the next year. When Parliament acted in the midst of a classic merger movement a generation later, the American experience had produced both a substantial justification of tight combinations on the basis of efficiency and a demonstration of the difficulty of applying an antitrust law unqualified by a "rule of reason." In neither period had Canadian legislators faced the "trust" question in ways that it was commonly posed in the United States: in 1889 there were no incorporated "trusts" in Canada to alarm the public, only comparatively harmless trade associations and local price-fixing conspiracies; by 1910 Canada did have companies that looked like trusts, but now the quasi-monopolistic corporation was defensible on the ground of efficiency, indeed for a Canadian "progressive" like Mackenzie King the giant corporation was a sign of healthy economic progress.

Nationalistic Canadian historians might be tempted to range further in the attempt to establish Canadian-American divergences and second Richard Hofstader's suggestion that antitrust legislation is "characteristically American." [35] Perhaps the extremely weak anti-combines movement in Canada reflected a weaker Canadian cultural and political commitment to the idea of competition as an economic or social good. From the days of the great fur-trading companies through the nation-building epic of the Canadian Pacific Railway, national economic development seemed to be in large measure a function of large-scale corporate enterprise. A considerably more conservative society than the United States, Canada

---

[34] Montreal Board of Trade Archives, Montreal Wholesale Grocers' Association, *Minutes*, July 15, 1910; September 12, November 2, 1911; *Canada Lumberman*, December 1, 1910; Herbert Gordon Stapells, "The Recent Consolidation Movement in Canadian Industry" (unpublished M. A. thesis, University of Toronto, 1920).

[35] "What Happened to the Antitrust Movement?", in *The Paranoid Style in American Politics and Other Essays* (New York, 1967), 195.

had no Jefferson, no Jacksonian age, no strong traditions of individualism and egalitarianism, not even in 1889 a very deep commitment to political democracy. Perhaps, then, this complex of cultural and economic factors made Canada rather more like Britain in its willingness to accommodate the thrust of business away from competition and towards collective organization. The "Tory touch" given Canadian history by the United Empire Loyalists affected even Canadian economic policy in the age of industrialism.[36]

But easy generalizations like these ignore substantial Canadian anti-monopoly and anti-corporation movements in areas other than national competition policy. To the western farmer of the 1880s and 1890s, for example, there was no greater soulless, bloodsucking, grinding octopus than the Canadian Pacific Railway. Manitobans were driven to threats of secession in the mid-1880s until the federal government rescinded the clause in the CPR charter granting it a twenty-year monopoly on western traffic. In 1902 the Laurier government responded to railway shippers' pressure by establishing the Board of Railway Commissioners as the Canadian equivalent of the Interstate Commerce Commission. On a municipal level there were numerous running battles between private utility corporations and municipal governments, leading in many cases to municipal ownership and to provincial ownership of telephones in Western Canada and of hydro-electric power in Ontario. Canadians did wrestle with their "corporation question," often as fiercely as Americans, but usually in ways that did not bring anti-combines legislation into play.

Of course the accidental 1900 change in the wording of the old Wallace Act had also partly muted demands for anti-combines legislation by giving the courts some authority to deal with the worst excesses of combines almost in spite of the legislators. Also, when there were clear instances of predatory monopolies which could not be reached by existing legislation, Parliament could be quick to respond: in 1904 Members of Parliament ceremonially denounced all trusts and amended the Inland Revenue Act to prevent the American Tobacco Company from monopolizing the manufacture of cigarettes in Canada through the use of exclusive contracts.[37]

[36] For interpretations stressing these themes in Canadian history, see, among others, Louis Hartz, ed., *The Founding of New Societies* (New York, 1964); Gad Horowitz, *Canadian Labour in Politics* (Toronto, 1968); H. A. Innis, *Essays in Canadian Economic History* (Toronto, 1956).

[37] House of Commons, *Debates*, August 4, 1904, 8394–8434; August 5, 8534–8550. This incident also demonstrated a clear tendency of Canadians to identify the trust as a particularly American phenomenon. It was common knowledge that the use of exclusive contracts was almost universal in Canadian business, and the amendment apparently

Finally, by far the most persistent economic issue in Canadian federal politics from 1879 to at least 1911 was the question of the tariff, the restrictionist device on which much of the Canadian manufacturing sector rested. Through most of these years the tariff sopped up much anti-monopoly sentiment which might otherwise have been concentrated on the combines issue, because it was seen by many as the legislative foundation of most Canadian combines. Had the Liberals and the Liberal press not so insistently linked combines with the tariff in 1889, for example, they might have forced the government to pass a reasonably strict anti-combines act.

Between 1889 and 1910, the structure of the Canadian economy and the ways in which problems of competition policy were presented to Canadian legislators at specific times, determined that "trust-busting" *per se* would be a minor and relatively insignificant aspect of government economic policy. In 1888, in the midst of a minor flurry of concern about combines, Canadians may have been first in the field with a bill symbolically headed "a bill to punish trusts." But it became "An Act to Declare the Common Law," and whatever historians finally conclude about the American anti-trust tradition in its formative years, it is misleading to suggest that Canadian governments had taken anti-combines policy seriously.

---

covered all uses of these contracts, but the government had no intention of using its legislation against any domestic manufacturer, and did not.

By T. W. Acheson

ASSOCIATE PROFESSOR OF HISTORY

UNIVERSITY OF NEW BRUNSWICK

Changing Social Origins of the Canadian Industrial Elite, 1880-1910

❡ *Professor Acheson presents the collective social portraits of two groups of leading Canadian industrialists, one from the years 1880–1885 and the other from 1905–1910. He considers such factors as ethnic and religious traditions, birthplaces, education, family backgrounds, career patterns, political and social activities, economic mobility, and regional differentials in analyzing the changing composition of the two elites.*

The period between 1879 and World War I witnessed a revolution in the structure and nature of Canadian industrial entrepreneurship.[1] The leading industrial firms of 1880 had, for the most part, been small family or partnership concerns valued at one or two hundred thousand dollars, usually employing up to a few hundred workers, and more often than not located in the nation's smaller towns and cities. By 1910 the joint stock company had become the dominant industrial form, and the tradition of a highly personal and often patriarchal rule which had characterized the proprietorship was gradually retreating in the face of the more impersonal company directorates and their subordinate hierarchy of career executives. Such rapid structural changes produced a significant impact on the group of men which dominated the nation's industrial life. It is this group or, more precisely, the changes and continuities which occurred within this group, that is the subject of this paper.

To achieve this end, an attempt has been made to identify most of the leading Canadian industrialists at the beginning and the end of the period under study. For purposes of this discussion these

Business History Review, Vol. XLVII, No. 2 (Summer, 1973). Copyright © The President and Fellows of Harvard College.

[1] For a detailed examination of this phenomenon, see my doctoral thesis, "The Social Origins of Canadian Industrialism: A Study in the Structure of Entrepreneurship 1880–1910" (University of Toronto, 1971), chapters 2–5. The changes in industrial structure parallelled a dramatic growth of Canada's industrial capability and of its industrial output. The real value of output increased from $423,000,000 in 1880 to $1,527,000,000 in 1910. See Gordon Bertram, "Historical Statistics on Growth and Structure in Manufacturing in Canada 1870–1957," J. Henripen and A. A. Asimakopulos, eds., *Canadian Political Science Association Conference on Statistics 1962 and 1963 Papers* (Toronto, 1964), 103.

two groups are referred to as the industrial elites of 1880–1885 and of 1905–1910. An effort then has been made to draw out collective social portraits of these two groups through examination of a number of factors in the background and life style of their members, including ethnic and religious traditions, birthplaces, educational attainments, family background, career patterns, and political, philanthropic, and social activities. The results of an analysis of the 1880–1885 elite have already been published.[2] This present study will examine the 1905–1910 elite with particular reference to the changes which are evident between the two groups. In many respects, these studies parallel those of Frances W. Gregory and Irene D. Neu,[3] and William Miller,[4] in the United States. Yet they differ from them in three important aspects. In the first place, the term "industrialist" is used in this study to refer only to those figures who played leading roles within the manufacturing sector; they sometimes may have been significant figures in other fields of economic activity as well, but they are included in one of these elites only if they were promoters, directors, officers, or operating personnel of some significant manufacturing enterprise.

In the second place, the members of the elites examined in this study were chosen in a less systematic fashion than were those dealt with by Gregory and Neu. The 168 individuals in the 1885 elite and the 231 in that of 1910 were selected arbitrarily from among those who owned, managed, or were on the boards of leading manufacturing firms. Selection of the earlier sample was comparatively simple: since control of most firms rested in the hands of a single owner, it was largely a matter of establishing the identity of the leading concerns of the early 1880's. Because of the structural changes which occurred in the intervening generation, the selection of the later elite became a much more complex problem. Through the medium of the trade journals — notably *The Monetary Times* and *Industrial Canada* — an attempt was made to establish which individuals played the leading roles in the promotion, direction, or management of major Canadian manufacturing concerns. These impressions were then confirmed by reference to the *Annual Financial Review*, to the existing studies of specific Canadian industries, and to available biographical data. The businessmen so selected

[2] David S. Macmillan, ed., *Canadian Business History: Selected Studies 1497–1971* (Toronto, 1972), 144–174.

[3] "The American Industrial Elite in the 1870's: Their Social Origins," in William Miller, ed., *Men in Business* (Cambridge, Mass., 1952), 191–211.

[4] "The American Business Elite: A Collective Portrait," *Journal of Economic History*, IX, 184–208.

came from a wide variety of manufacturing industries. While no attempt was made to bias the sample in this regard, the most rapidly expanding industries — notably textiles — necessarily received greater emphasis than their actual output might seem to merit. Thus members of the earlier elite were found in about equal numbers (each between one-fifth and one-quarter of the total) in the forest products, secondary iron and steel, and textile industries. Smaller numbers were found in the food products, leather products, and paper industries. The same elements were present in the later elite, although the proportion of each had been somewhat reduced.[5] In addition, the later elite contained a number of representatives of the "new industries," notably primary iron and steel and electrical products.

Finally, unlike the work of Gregory and Neu, this study gives considerable emphasis to regional factors in the analysis of the elites of 1880–1885 and 1905–1910. To assess the latter, the country has been divided into four rough geographic regions: the Maritime provinces of the eastern seaboard, the St. Lawrence Valley including Quebec and eastern Ontario, the Lake Peninsula of Ontario, and finally the vast pioneer area extending from Lake Superior to British Columbia, a region which has been designated as the West.

I

While many of the firms of 1880 had seen their ownership diffused through the new financial capitalism, the manufacturer[6] still frequently played a major and often dominant role in both the policy-making and administrative affairs of many of the older leading industrial firms of 1910. In firms, such as Massey and Harris, which had been transformed into joint stock companies, individual families were usually still able to dominate corporate proceedings. Even in many of the new industrial concerns there was not the clear-cut division between capital and management which Arthur Cole and Ralf Dahrendorff typify as the hallmark of a fully mature industrial organization.[7] While the salaried career executive was

[5] Since many of these men were actively involved in the affairs of several different types of industrial enterprises, it becomes much more difficult to generalize about the types of industries represented in this sample.

[6] The term "manufacturer" has been applied in this study only to those owner-managers whose principal work centered on the day-to-day administration of a manufacturing concern. Thus manufacturers are industrialists, but many other industrialists participated in the industrial process only as promoters or as members of corporate directorates.

[7] Arthur H. Cole, *Business Enterprise in Its Social Setting* (Cambridge, Mass., 1959), 187–205; Ralf Dahrendorff, *Class and Class Conflict in Industrial Society* (Stanford, Cal., 1959), 44–47.

a growing phenomenon in most companies, the leading executives in many firms were also directors of the corporation who usually possessed large stock holdings in their own right.[8] Indeed, in many companies the British tradition prevailed — the president fulfilled the function of a board chairman and management of the concern fell to one of the other corporate directors, usually referred to as the managing director. Hence by 1910 manufacturers were still a significant part of the industrial elite although, increasingly, their traditional roles as promoters and directors of manufacturing enterprises were being usurped by leaders from a variety of other business activities.

TABLE 1

PRIMARY OCCUPATION OF THE INDUSTRIALISTS

	1885 Elite	1910 Elite
Manufacturer	85%	58%
Wholesaler	9	12
Broker	—	6
Shipper	1	5
Contractor	—	4
Transportation Executive	2	4
Financier	—	3
Financial Executive	1	3
Other	2	4
Total	100	100
Total Cases	168[a]	231[a]

[a] In subsequent tables the sample sizes will vary from topic to topic depending on the availability of data. Biographical data on the subjects in this study were gathered from a number of monographs dealing with individual families, from several trade journals and newspapers — particularly *The Canadian Manufacturer, Industrial Canada, The Monetary Times* — and from a number of biographical dictionaries. The most notable of the latter include: G. M. Rose, ed., *The Cyclopedia of Canadian Biography* (2 volumes, Toronto, 1886, 1888), hereafter cited as *CCB*; *Encyclopedia of Canadian Biography* (3 volumes, Montreal, 1904, 1905, 1907), hereafter cited as *ECB*; G. M. Adams, ed., *Prominent Men* (Toronto, 1892); Henry J. Morgan, ed., *Canadian Men and Women of the Time* (Toronto, 1898, 1912), hereafter cited as *CMWT* (1898) and *CMWT* (1912); William H. Atherton, *Montreal* (Montreal, 1914), III; C. W. Parker, ed., *Who's Who and Why* (Toronto, 1914), V, hereafter cited as *WWW*, V; C. W. Parker, ed., *Who's Who and Why* (*West*) (Vancouver, 1913), III, cited hereafter as *WWW* (*West*).

The presence of these large numbers of non-manufacturers within the industrial elite was a reflection of the extent to which the nature of industrial entrepreneurship had been altered by the structural changes that had occurred in the financial and administrative organization of the firm. Nowhere was this more evident than in the

[8] For example, Frank Meighan was the long-time treasurer and a director of the Lake of the Woods Milling Company, a firm of which his father had been the co-founder and president; Charles Riordon was vice-president and managing director of his family firm, Riordon Pulp and Paper.

consolidation movement, which had given control of a large number of producing units in a variety of industries across vast geographical reaches to a relatively small group of industrialists centered in Montreal. The impact of this change was reflected in the growing numbers of Montreal businessmen within the ranks of the leading Canadian industrialists, a development which gave the St. Lawrence region a decisive advantage over the more heavily industrialized Lake Peninsula.

Regardless of their occupation or their region of residence, the industrialists of 1910 were drawn largely from the ranks of the native-born. As Table 3 illustrates, this represented a dramatic change from 1885. The decline of the non-native-born was not, however, distributed proportionally among the several national groups. The Scots, by far the most significant non-Canadian element in the earlier elite, were reduced to one-third their former influence, while the Irish, the German, and the American-born were

TABLE 2
REGIONAL DISTRIBUTION OF THE INDUSTRIAL ELITE

	1885 Elite	1910 Elite
Maritimes	19%	12%
St. Lawrence	40	49
Lake Peninsula	37	27
The West	4	12
Total	100	100
Total Cases	168	231

TABLE 3
BIRTHPLACES OF THE INDUSTRIAL ELITE

Native-Born:	1885 Elite	1910 Elite
Maritimes	18%	12%
St. Lawrence	} 33	31
Lake Peninsula		30
The West	0	1
Non-Native-Born:		
Scotland	20	7
Ireland (Prot.)	} 7	3
Ireland (Cath.)		1
England	6	7
United States	12	7
Germany	4	1
Total	100	100
Total Cases	164	227

also significantly less important by 1910. Only among the English-born had this trend been halted.

There were, however, marked regional differences in the birth-places of the industrialists of 1910. The proportion of non-native-born varied from nine out of ten in the Maritimes to less than seven in ten in the St. Lawrence and Western regions (see Table 4). The

TABLE 4

MIGRATION AND INDUSTRIAL OPPORTUNITY BY REGION IN 1910

	Maritimes	St. Lawrence	Lake Peninsula	The West
Birthplaces of Native-born:				
Maritimes	85%	3%	—%	7%
St. Lawrence	4	57	3	14
Lake Peninsula	—	7	74	46
The West	—	2	—	—
Birthplaces of Non-Native-born:				
Scotland	4	11	3	4
England	7	5	6	17
Ireland	—	5	5	4
United States	—	9	9	4
Germany	—	1	—	4
Total	100	100	100	100
Number of Cases	28	111	63	28

most surprising change occurred in the Lake Peninsula, where the native-born rose from less than two-fifths of the group of 1885 to nearly three-quarters of that of 1910. Intra-regional migration was not nearly as significant a source of leading industrialists as was international migration, but it is significant that nearly half the western elite had been born in the Lake Peninsula and only one in five in the remainder of Canada.

The reason for this rapidly changing demographic pattern among the entrepreneurs of eastern Canada is probably found in the changing scope and pattern of immigration to Canada in the mid-nineteenth century. Most of the leading industrialists of 1885 had been born between 1820 and 1840, and they had been swept into North America as part of a tidal wave of British immigration that had shaped the society of the British colonies, particularly that of Upper Canada, in the generation before 1850. By contrast, most of the entrepreneurs of 1910 had been born between 1845 and 1870, as the immigrant tide receded, and they were the sons of immigrants rather than immigrants themselves. They tended to reflect the changing composition of this declining immigration and the less fluid society which it produced. Thus the migrant portion of the elite fell to one-quarter of the group, and even the composition of this fragment differed substantially from that of the previous generation. In the course of the 1850s and 1860s, the dominant Irish and Scottish streams dramatically declined and were replaced by a steadily growing movement of English migration, which reached its peak in the early twentieth century.[9] Scottish-born industrialists, who had outnumbered their English counterparts nearly four to one in 1885, were barely able to maintain parity with them by 1910, while in the Lake Peninsula and the West they were rapidly outnumbered by the incoming tide. On the other hand, most leading entrepreneurs were native-born sons of British immigrants of the 1820–1850 period, and among this group the older Scottish and Irish traditions remained unchallenged. In fact, the birthplace of the fathers of the industrial leaders of 1910 closely paralleled that of the leading industrialists of 1885.

The continued importance of immigrants among the entrepreneurs of the St. Lawrence region highlighted a cogent social difference between the St. Lawrence and the Lake Peninsula. The immigrant who ultimately achieved status as an industrialist in the former region had rarely ever been just an aspect of a mass migration (as frequently had been the case in the latter). With a few

TABLE 5

BIRTHPLACES OF FATHERS OF THE INDUSTRIAL ELITE

	1885 Elite	1910 Elite
Native-born:		
Maritimes	13%	9%
St. Lawrence	9	10
Lake Peninsula		8
Non-Native-born:		
Scotland	28	30
Ireland (Prot.)	14	11
Ireland (Cath.)	3	5
England	13	17
United States	15	8
Germany	5	2
Total	100	100
Total Cases	151	175

[9] The English-born population of Canada rose from 144,999 in 1871 to 519,401 in 1911. The Scottish-born declined from 121,074 in 1871 to 83,631 in 1901, then rose to 169,391 during the next decade. The Irish-born declined from 224,422 in 1871 to 92,874 in 1911. Canada, *Census* (1911), III, ix.

notable exceptions, the Montreal immigrant idustrialists had arrived in the city to fill a specific vocational need or opportunity. When the Celtic migration tapered off after 1850, the Scottish or Irish-born entrepreneur also ceased to appear in the Lake Peninsula but did continue to gravitate to the city of Montreal — sometimes on his own initiative, but more often in conjunction with one of the many Scottish enterprises in that city.[10] Within Montreal, the Canadian Pacific Railway, the Hudson's Bay Company, and the Bank of Montreal bristled with a whole panoply of first and second generation Scots.[11]

On the other hand, the Lake Peninsula experience, with its immigrant English and second generation Celtic elite, was repeated in the Canadian West, where the Ontario hegemony proved to have very fragile roots. The Ontario-born industrial leaders of the new West came not from the "old" Ontario population — Loyalist and post-Loyalist American — but from the "new": they were almost entirely sons of Irish and Scottish immigrants.[12]

Whether native-born or of immigrant origins, the industrialist of 1910, like his predecessor of 1885, was the product of a defined social tradition which was usually embodied in the rites and assumptions of one or more religious denominations. Yet the strength

[10] Thus William Cantlie, the dry goods wholesaler who eventually became a leading woolens manufacturer, came to Montreal from Aberdeen in 1863 to work as a clerk for William Stephen, a Scot and a leading dry goods wholesaler. Similarly, the twenty-one year-old James Wilson, who was to become a director of five major steel industries, was brought to Montreal in 1871 in conjunction with the wholesale metals firm of Thos. Robertson & Company. Within five years the young man assumed the managing directorship of that firm. *ECB*, I, 40; *CMWT* (1912), 1176.

[11] Among the more prominent members of this group were Lord Strathcona, who dominated the Railway and controlled the Hudson's Bay Company; his cousin, Lord Mount Stephen, who headed both the Railway and the Bank; the son of the former chief factor of the Hudson's Bay Company, Sir Edward Clouston, who rose to the general managership of the Bank of Montreal and sat as a director of nine major industrial firms including the three largest iron and steel manufactories in the city of Montreal. It included as well the Montreal wholesaler and Canadian Pacific Railway vice-president Duncan McIntyre and his sons who headed several Montreal textile firms; R. B. Angus, the Scottish bank clerk who became part of the C.P.R. syndicate, president of the Bank, and leading industrialist; Senator James Ross, the Cromarty engineer who supervised construction of the western division of the C.P.R. and who was to become perhaps the foremost industrialist in the nation, and Ross' son, John, who followed his father into a variety of industrial enterprises. They were joined by Lord Mount Stephen's cousin-in-law James Cantlie, and by his brother-in-law, the Scotch-Irishman, Robert Meighan, who came to Montreal in association with Mount Stephen in 1879 and founded the Lake-of-the-Woods Milling Company; and Meighan's son, Frank who followed his father into a variety of flour, railroad, and woolens firms.

For brief biographical sketches of the above see the following: on Lord Mount Stephen, Heather Gilbert, *Awakening Continent: The Life of Lord Mount Stephen* (Aberdeen, 1965); on Lord Strathcona, H. Beckles Willson, *The Life of Lord Strathcona and Mount Royal* (Boston, 1915); on Sir Edward Clouston, *Montreal*, III, 32–37, *Monetary Times*, August 20, 1892, and *CMWT* (1912), 241; on Duncan McIntyre, *Industrial Canada* (July, 1904), *CMWT* (1912), 772; on James Cantlie, *ECB*, II, 40, *CCB*, I, 746, *CMWT* (1898), 153, *CMWT* (1912), 198, and *WWW*, V, 176; on Robert Meighan, *Montreal*, III, 74–80; on R. B. Angus, *Montreal*, III, 5–8, *ECB*, I, 9, *CCB*, II, 465–66, and *CMWT* (1912), 29.

[12] The exception to this generalization, C. A. Flumerfelt, was the grandson of Ontario United Empire Loyalists.

of these ethnic traditions differed significantly between the two groups, if for no other reason than that the later industrialists were typically a generation further removed from the source of the traditions, and their attachment to the ethnic character was an act of faith and sentiment rather than one of conformity. Even so, ethnicity did continue to provide the basis for a ritual of identification. The dominant characteristic in this ethnic pattern was the continuing strength of the Celtic traditions as a whole, traditions which were strengthened in the period at the expense of the North American ones. Between 1885 and 1910, the American element in the industrial elite declined significantly, while the other North American traditions — the French and the Loyalist — remained relatively stable. By contrast, British groups increased from little more than two-fifths to nearly three-quarters of the group.

TABLE 6

PATERNAL ETHNIC ORIGINS OF THE INDUSTRIAL ELITE

	1885 Elite	1910 Elite	General Population in 1911
Scottish	32%	34%	14%
English	13	21	26
Irish (Prot.)	14	13	} 15
Irish (Cath.)	3	5	
American	22	13	—[a]
Loyalist	5	5	—[a]
French	7	6	29
German/Swiss	4	3	6
Total	100	100	90[b]
Total Cases	155	178	7,206,000

[a] Americans were considered, for census purposes, as belonging to one of the European traditions.
[b] The remaining 10 per cent included a variety of ethnic groups, of which the Ukrainian, Dutch, and Polish were the largest.

Of the several British traditions among the leading industrialists of 1910, those of the Scots and the Irish Catholics most successfully survived into the second generation. The Englishman and the Irish Protestant, by contrast, appear to have integrated most quickly into the society at large. The Scottish national societies — the St. Andrew, the Caledonian, and the North British — thrived to a remarkable degree among both the first and second generation Scottish industrialists of Montreal, as did the United Irish League among Toronto's Catholic group. The Montreal St. Andrews' Society alone claimed the allegiance of no fewer than ten leading industrialists. By contrast, apparently not a single native Canadian industrialist of English or Irish Protestant origins belonged to any distinctively national organization. Nor did any Irish Protestant of any generation acknowledge membership in the Orange Lodge. Similarly, while most French-Canadian industrialists belonged to specific French-Canadian organizations, such as Montreal's Chambre de Commerce, L'Alliance française, or the several private French clubs in Montreal, none publicly claimed membership in distinctive national organizations such as the Saint-Jean-Baptiste Society.

Ethnic traditions tended to be institutionalized in the several denominations through which Canadians gave expression to their world-view. With few exceptions, these denominations in 1910 reflected the ethnic changes that had occurred in the composition of the elite in the previous generation. The Anglican (Episcopalian) element within the group experienced a significant growth; most other denominations, and particularly those whose roots were essentially North American, declined.

TABLE 7
RELIGION OF THE INDUSTRIAL ELITE

	1885 Elite	1910 Elite	General Population in 1911
Presbyterian	36%	33%	15%
Anglican	19	27	15
Methodist	19	17	15
Roman Catholic	12	12	40
Baptist	6	5	5
Congregationalist	4	1.5	.5
Other Protestant	4	4	7
Jewish	0	.5	1
Total	100	100	98.5[a]
Total Cases	138	202	7,206,000

[a] Other categories 1.5 per cent.

The persistence of the traditional ethnic denominational loyalties was particularly evident in the Maritime and the St. Lawrence regions. Here virtually all the Irish Protestants, even unto the third generation, remained within the Anglican or Presbyterian communions; all those of French origins remained within the Roman Catholic fold. The Scots provided the best example of the continuity of the religious and ethnic tradition: not only did virtually all first generation Scots throughout the country claim the Presbyterian faith, but so did more than six-sevenths of the second generation Scottish-Canadians.[13]

The situation was reversed in the Lake Peninsula. There, the evangelical churches — notably the Methodist and the Baptist — survived, as they had traditionally done, through their ability to attract converts from the immigrant traditions. The Methodists, for example, attracted none of the immigrants among the regional elite, yet they commanded the allegiance of every second generation Irish Protestant in both the Lake Peninsula and the West, of nearly every second and third generation American-Canadian in both regions, and with the Baptists challenged the Anglican hegemony among those of English origins.[14] This development was most significant. Since most of the leading Methodist industrialists of the 1880s had been of post-Loyalist American descent, the decline of this element among the industrial elite of the next generation — the Masseys were a notable exception — destroyed almost all continuity among the Methodist element in the elite. The Methodists in the later elite were mostly the sons of British immigrants. Indeed, the degree to which Methodism had itself become an expression of a regional culture was revealed among the industrial entrepreneurs of the western region. Most of the latter were sons of British immigrants who had settled in Ontario, yet by 1910, their presence in the West gave the Methodists a commanding position in the western elite.

Indeed, among the industrial elite of the Lake Peninsula the close

TABLE 8

RELIGION OF THE INDUSTRIAL ELITE OF 1910 BY REGION

	Maritimes	St. Lawrence	Lake Peninsula	West
Presbyterian	33%	41%	20%	28%
Anglican	33	25	26	20
Methodist	15	4	28	44
Roman Catholic	4	20	6	8
Baptist	11	1	11	0
Congregationalist	4	2	2	0
Other Protestant	0	6	6	0
Jewish	0	1	0	0
Total	100	100	100	100
Total Number	27	97	53	25

[13] Only two did not, one of whom was a Congregationalist, the other a Unitarian.
[14] Methodists and Baptists together equalled the Anglican following among the second generation English-Canadian industrialists of the Lake Peninsula.

relationship between ethnicity and religion appears by 1910 to have been well on the way to disintegration among most British and Protestant traditions. The aggressively evangelical denominations such as the Methodists had provided much of the impetus to this development, but that was true, as well, of the Church of England. The greatest strength of the latter denomination, for example, was not among the English-born industrialists, but among the "new" Americans — executives sent as managers of Canadian branch plants [15] — and from among the converts made from other Protestant churches.[16] This tendency was particularly pronounced among the Halifax elite, where three small-town emigrants to the city [17] all entered the Anglican faith. The whole movement suggests the emergence of a system built upon some measure of denominational and class indentification, with Anglicans and Presbyterians entering the more evangelical churches at the lower end of the social system and, by a process of gradual osmosis, moving back again at the higher status levels.

Inherited traditions, however, provide only one insight into the background of the industrial entrepreneur of 1910. Equally as important was the physical environment in which he was raised and the preparation which he brought to his career. Nothing, perhaps, more distinguished the leading industrialists of 1910 from their counterparts of the previous generation than the educational levels achieved by the former. More than three-quarters of the 164 individuals on whom information is available had attended high

TABLE 9

EDUCATION OF THE INDUSTRIAL ELITE

	1885 Elite	1910 Elite
None	4%	1%
Common School	55	23
High School	36	61
College	5	15
Total	100	100
Total Cases	122	164

[15] Every American-born member of the Lake Peninsula elite was an Anglican in 1910.

[16] Notable examples of this phenomenon were W. O. Matthews, scion of a prominent Toronto Methodist family, and Lloyd Harris, a fourth generation Brantford Baptist, both of whom entered the Anglican faith. *CCB*, I, 340–41; *CMWT* (1912), 743; *CMWT* (1912), 504.

[17] J. W. Allison, a nephew of the Methodist founder of Mount Allison University, Mr. Justice Robert Harris, an Annapolis Baptist, and Falmouth lawyer and Acadia University graduate, John Payzant; see *CMWT* (1912), 19; *CMWT* (1912), 505; *CCB*, II, 778; *CMWT* (1898), 810.

school or college, and the proportion was even higher among those born after 1860.

There was, however, considerable variation in the educational attainments of the regional and occupational groups which comprised the 1910 elite. Non-manufacturers among the industrialists were better educated than manufacturers, and immigrants tended to have a somewhat poorer education than natives, although, significantly, younger immigrants were often among the best-educated members of the elite, confirming again the hypothesis that the migrants of the late nineteenth century arrived not as part of a mass migration but in response to specific vocational needs which they were peculiarly trained to fill. Among the native-born industrialists, there was little difference in the educational standards of those from the three eastern regions. However, the contrast between the eastern regions and the West was striking. In the latter case nearly half the industrialists possessed only a common school education, a situation reminiscent of the Lake Peninsula group a generation earlier.

Another characteristic which distinguished the industrialist of 1910 from his counterpart of the 1880s was the presence of the private school graduate in the ranks of the former. This phenomenon was particularly evident among the financial industrialists of the Anglican faith in the Toronto area, but even this generalization was being swept away as Presbyterians [18] and Baptists [19] sent their sons off to Upper Canada College. The practice had become most prevalent among ambitious small-scale businessmen and manufacturers in the last half of the nineteenth century, and by 1900 it had cut across all religious, occupational, and geographic lines. Among those members of the elite born after 1860, about one-third appear to have been products of private educational systems.

Still, while the private school graduate constituted only a small part of the whole elite — about one in nine — he was symptomatic of the general rise in the educational level of the entire group. And while most industrialists born after 1860 had not attended private schools, the overwhelming majority of them, from all social origins, had attended a public high school. Indeed, Montreal High School rather than Upper Canada College was the nursery of the Canadian industrialists of 1910.[20]

[18] Such as the Ottawa lumber manufacturer, James MacLaren; see *CMWT* (1912), 705.

[19] Such as the Parry Sound lumberman, John Miller. *ECB*, II, 58.

[20] There were twenty alumni of Montreal High School and eight of Upper Canada College in the 1910 elite.

The most important factor precipitating this change in educational levels seems to have been the urban origins of the industrialists. Every one of the Montreal-born industrialists, for example, had at least begun a secondary education. By contrast, most of the St. Lawrence entrepreneurs who had spent their childhoods in a rural setting received only a common school education. A similar situation obtained in the Lake Peninsula, the single crucial difference being that here most entrepreneurs had received their secondary education in the numerous grammar schools located in dozens of small Ontario cities and country towns such as Dundas, Beamsville, Barrie, Georgetown, Seaforth, Brantford, Peterborough, Galt, Woodstock, Oakville, and Lindsay. By 1910 about four of every five Canadian industrialists on whom information is available were products of an urban or semi-urban environment. Those of the St. Lawrence — whether native or immigrant — were largely from city backgrounds; those of the other three regions were from small provincial towns. Most had been reared in these communities between 1850 and 1880, at a time when the population of the nation as a whole, even at the later date, was nearly 75 per cent rural.

TABLE 10

EDUCATION LEVEL ACHIEVED BY MEMBERS OF THE INDUSTRIAL
ELITE OF 1910, BY SIZE OF CHILDHOOD COMMUNITY

Community	Education					
	None	Common School	High School	College	Total	Number
Rural (%)	3	47	20	20	100	30
Town a (%)	—	21	74	5	100	58
City (%)	—	12	67	21	100	76

a Because of the difficulties involved in identifying the size of any Canadian town before 1871, any community which was deemed a local center of the period has been considered as a "town" for purposes of this table.

Having acquired their education, most of the industrial leaders of 1910 moved into the business world while still in their late teens. The early career patterns of these men contrasted sharply with those of their predecessors of 1885. The most obvious distinction between the two was the presence among the former of a group of young men, found largely in Montreal, who inherited substantial resources from their fathers and effectively began their careers as capitalists.[21] About half of all the industrialists of 1910 entered

21 The contrast was illustrated in the career of Sir Hugh Allan, who left his Scottish

businesses — manufacturing, mercantile, financial, transportation, or construction firms — which were owned or controlled by their fathers or uncles. Some of these concerns were already large joint stock corporations; most were relatively small family firms which were used as a base from which the entrepreneur later expanded his activities. Most of the remaining industrialists, and particularly those of more limited means, began their careers in the service of one of the joint stock companies.

Regardless of which avenue a young man followed, his road to material success was most likely to bring him ultimately into one of the four or five major metropolitan centers. The most successful entrepreneur would almost certainly end his career in Montreal or Toronto. Of these two centers, Montreal had benefited most from the structural changes which had revolutionized the structure of Canadian industry in the previous generation. That city's industrial influence was measured not in what its entrepreneurs possessed, but in what they controlled; the latter probably constituted the greater part of the Canadian industrial machine in 1910.

Aside from the question of industrial influence, the Montreal and Toronto entrepreneurs reflected marked social differences. The Montreal industrial community tended to be much more cosmopolitan in taste and outlook than was its relatively staid and limited Toronto counterpart. As Table 11 illustrates, the Montrealer tended to be an urban creature, often a product of the St. Lawrence metropolis itself; or if not from that city, usually an immigrant from a British or an American urban background. The industrial community of Montreal was not socially a part of the region which it dominated; it tended to find its members either within the narrow confines of the English-speaking community, or to recruit them from outside the region. Hence the ties and loyalties of its members were diffuse and usually extra-regional. It was perhaps not surprising, then, that the imperial federation movement found its strength among the city's powerful Irish Protestant industrialists, or that the ethnic and denominational traditions persisted so successfully in the region, or even that the imperial military traditions were most faithfully preserved among the Montreal industrialists.[22] The life

common school to work as a clerk at the age of twelve, and who was forty-two before he assumed control of his own firm, and that of his son, Sir Montagu Allan, who, after completing his education at Bishops College school and at Paris, entered the Allan Steamship Company as a principal officer and owner at the age of twenty one. He succeeded his father to the directorates of major rubber, paper, steel products, and textile manufactories. *CCB,* 35–36; *CBC,* II, 7–10; *Monetary Times,* December 15, 1882; *ECB,* I, 16; *CMWT* (1912), 15; *Montreal,* III, 660–662.

[22] Most of the militia officers among the industrial elite were found in Montreal.

style of its leading figures was secular, gregarious, and catholic in its interests, a fact reflected in the variety of Montreal's elite clubs, which numbered at least thirty-two to Toronto's fourteen. By contrast, the smaller Toronto industrial community was largely peopled by migrants from the surrounding hinterlands, and it reflected the sober methodistic environment of the rural and small-town Lake Peninsula from which most of its entrepreneurs had come. The latter gave a puritan air to the city's business community, an atmosphere manifested in the external interests and religious concerns of so many of its entrepreneurs, and in its more limited secular, cultural, and recreational pursuits. In this respect Montreal played the metropolitan thesis to Toronto's frontierist antithesis.

And indeed the migration pattern which characterized the early career of the Toronto industrialist was emulated on a smaller scale by the other regional Canadian centers of 1910. Only in the Maritimes did more than one-third of the regional elite live outside the major regional centers. With the exception of Montreal, most of the leading industrialists in all of these cities were migrants.

In retrospect, then, the typical industrial leader of 1910 was an American or British immigrant, or, more likely, the son of a British immigrant. Although he was still likely to have been raised in a Scottish Presbyterian tradition, the primacy of this group within the industrial elite was being challenged by a growing English and Anglican element. The product of an urban or small-town environment, he acquired, for the period, an uncommonly adequate education before gravitating to one of a half-dozen metropolitan centers — but particularly to Montreal or Toronto — in search of vocational opportunities. The career pattern which he followed, and particularly the degree of social mobility indicated in his rise to industrial prominence, is the next theme which will be examined.

II

Equally as significant as the shifts in the demographic origins of the industrial elites between 1885 and 1910 were changes in the social origins of their members. Nearly three-quarters of the 129 leading industrialists of 1910 for whom information is available were scions of business and professional families, a proportion that was significantly higher than in the 1885 elite. This fact, combined with the simultaneous decline of those from farm and workingmen's backgrounds, would seem to indicate a sharply reduced degree of social mobility at work within the industrial elite of 1910.

TABLE 11
CAREER PATTERNS OF THE 1910 ELITE: GEOGRAPHICAL STRUCTURES

	Maritimes		St. Lawrence			Lake Peninsula		West	
Outside Metro-Remained [a]	36%		4%			26%		—	
Outside Metro-Moved Outside [b]	4		1			1		—	
Entered Region-Outside Metro [c]	7		—			—		27%	
In Metro-Moved Out [d]	—		—			—		—	
	Halifax	St. John	Quebec	Montreal	Ottawa	Toronto	Hamilton	Winnipeg	Vancouver
Outside Metro-To Metro [e]	21	7	1	10	3	32	5	—	14
Entered Region-To Metro [f]	4	1	2	28	1	12	7	55	—
In Metro-Remained [g]	7	14	5	38	7	16	1	4	—
Total	100		100			100		100	
Total Cases	28		110			63		28	

[a] Began career in a community outside a major center, remained in that community throughout his career. The term "metro" indicates any one of the nine Canadian cities listed in the table.

[b] Began career outside a major center and later moved to another community within the region. At no time did he settle in a metro.

[c] Entered the region, usually from another country, in the pursuit of a career. Settled in a community outside a metro.

[d] Moved from a metro to another community in the region.

[e] Moved from a smaller regional community to a metro in the pursuit of a career.

[f] Entered the region, usually from another country, in the pursuit of a career. Settled in a metro.

[g] Usually a native of a metro. Began and continued his career there.

Indeed, there is much evidence to support this case for declining mobility. For one thing, a number of individuals in the 1910 elite were members of families which had produced leading manufacturers and other businessmen for two and even, occasionally, three generations.[23] There was, however, at least as much attrition as continuation among these old business families. After nearly a century in the flour industry, for example, the Ogilvie firm passed from the family in 1900 on the death of the third-generation miller, William Ogilvie, and it was acquired by a consortium headed by the firm's general manager, Frederick Thompson.[24] Ogilvie's son Albert, who was made a millionaire by his father's holdings, settled down to the life of a capitalist gentleman.[25]

A much greater degree of continuity was evident among families of second generation standing in the elite. At least fifty-three members of the elite of 1910 were clearly identifiable as sons of leading Canadian industrialists or merchants.[26] In addition to these, some

TABLE 12

FATHER'S OCCUPATION

	1885 Elite	1910 Elite
Professional	8%	15%
Businessman [a]	23	32
Manufacturer	32	28
Manager [b]	5	9
Farmer	26	15
Craftsman	6	1
Laborer	0	0
Total	100	100
Total Cases	105	129

[a] Includes shippers, construction, transportation and financial executives, bankers, wholesalers, and a few retailers.
[b] Includes sea captains, army officers, supervisory personnel in any institution, and most civil servants.

[23] The several families represented in the latter case included, among others, that of the agricultural implements manufacturer, Alanson Harris, of Brantford, whose grandson Lloyd left the company service in 1900 and achieved control of several industrial firms through his role as a financier; of John Redpath of Montreal, whose grandson, Huntley Redpath Drummond, succeeded his father, Sir George A. Drummond as head of the large St. Lawrence sugar refining industry; and of Henry Markland Molson, the Montreal capitalist whose grandfather had pioneered in the steam navigation of the St. Lawrence. For brief biographical sketches of the above see the following: on Lloyd Harris, *Men of Canada*, I, 154, *CMWT* (1912), 504; on Huntley Drummond, *Montreal*, III, 304, *CMWT* (1912), 345, *WWW* (V), 244; on Henry M. Molson, Merrill Denison, *The Barley and the Stream: The Molson Story* (Toronto, 1955), *CMWT* (1912), 814.
[24] *The Canadian Magazine*, XXII, 441–43; *Montreal*, III, 217–233.
[25] *CMWT* (1912), 864.
[26] Typical of these were Robert Hopper, the asbestos and cement producer, whose father had been a prominent Quebec cattle dealer, and Lorne McGibbon, the rubber and footwear baron, whose father was a leading Montreal merchant. *Montreal*, III, 428–430; *ECB*, II, 111.

twenty-one members of the 1885 elite remained among the 1910 industrialists. Still another indication of the hardening social fabric was the growing incidence of intermarriage among the offspring of leading entrepreneurs.[27] In all, at least fifteen marriages, each involving two leading industrial families, occurred among the members of the elites of 1885 and 1910.

Yet, even when all of the factors of continuity are considered, there remains evidence of a relatively high degree of social mobility in the formation of the 1910 elite. Less than 20 per cent of the group were directly associated with the leading industrialists of 1885. Moreover, most of these were not sons of manufacturers but generally were scions of great Montreal mercantile and transportation interests such as the Morrices, the Gaults, and particularly, the Allans.

The social mobility which enabled large numbers of hitherto unknown entrepreneurs to enter the elite at the turn of the century differed from that of the previous generation in that it tended to be less vertical and, hence, less spectacular. The most common form of mobility was accomplished over two generations through a type of diagonal, evolutionary movement on the part of a large number of young men whose businessmen fathers had operated modest mercantile or manufacturing firms in the 1870s and early 1880s. Building upon the resources garnered by their fathers, these ambitious entrepreneurs seized the opportunities offered through the new corporate financial structures, through the combination movement, or simply through expansion of an existing family firm to propel themselves into the front ranks of the industrial policy makers of the Dominion.[28]

[27] One such union, the marriage of David Morrice Jr. to the daughter of the daughter of Andrew Gault, united the two leading Montreal textile families. Another brought together the Montreal engineer, contractor and industrialist, Herbert Holt and the daughter of the Sherbrooke woolens manufacturer, Andrew Paton. In a similar union the iron and steel baron G. E. Drummond of Montreal married the daughter of Brantford agricultural implements manufactuer Ignatius Cockshutt, while Guelph industrialist Christian Kloepfer took as his bride the daughter of the Calgary meat packer, Patrick Burns. For brief biographical sketches of the above see the following: on David Morrice, Jr., ECB, I, 85, CMWT (1912), 821; on Andrew Gault, ECB, II, 13, The Canadian Magazine, XXI, 201–203; on Herbert Holt, CMWT (1898), 474, WWW (1914), 455; on Andrew Paton, CCB, II, 448, CBD, II, 314–15; on G. E. Drummond, ECB, I, 12, CMWT, (1912), 345, and Industrial Canada, May, 1904; on Christian Kloepfer, CMWT (1912), 619; and on Patrick Burns, A. F. Sproule, "The Role of Patrick Burns in the Development of Western Canada" (M. A. thesis, University of Alberta, 1962).

[28] The pattern is illustrated in the career of A. E. Dyment who, at the age of twenty-three, inherited a successful Simcoe County lumber firm from his father. Fourteen years later he disposed of the concern and established a Toronto brokerage through which medium he acquired an interest in a variety of industrial enterprises. A different path to success was adopted by Edmund Robert who, at the height of the consolidation movement, took his father's small Beauharnois woolen mill and used it as the basis for the Dominion Woolen Manufacturing Company, of which he became managing director. CMWT (1912), 359; CMWT (1912), 947.

The greatest opportunities for vertical mobility were provided by the major changes in industrial technology and in the new corporate structures. Chief among the former in the closing decades of the nineteenth century had been the expanding railroad system and the emerging electrical power industry.[29] Most important in the development of the new electrical industry was the role of technically skilled individuals, most of them immigrants who arrived in response to the need for specific technical ability. These included Frederic Nicholls (who was instrumental in forming Canadian General Electric), Ottawa electrical contractors Thomas Ahearn and Warren Soper, and the American company executives, Paul Myles and John Aldred.

An equally important vehicle of social mobility was provided through the cracks opened in the changing administrative and financial structure of the industrial corporation. Through the new opportunities provided by these ruptures at least three new groups of industrialists emerged — the career executive, the stock broker, and the lawyer. Each provided a specialized service necessary to the functioning of the corporate entity, and most were the products of humble origins. Among the lawyers, Hamilton's Sir John Gibson,[30] Montreal's James Greenshields [31] and Halifax's Mr. Justice Robert Harris,[32] were all involved in the promotion of a variety of new steel, electricity, and paper concerns, and they were all products of agrarian backgrounds. The situation was less clear among the stock brokers. Lloyd Harris, Sir Henry Pellatt,[33] and Edward Jarvis [34] were certainly scions of distinguished families, but Sir Edmund Osler,[35] Alfred Ames,[36] and Lord Beaverbrook [37] were all sons of undistinguished small-town clergymen, the Hanson brothers of Montreal were sons of a Cornish sea captain,[38] and

[29] The success stories in the former field of endeavor included those of the Canadian Pacific Railway's former general manager for construction, Senator James Ross, and his subordinates Sir Donald Mann and Sir William MacKenzie, both the sons of humble Scottish immigrants. All three went on to promote numerous iron and steel firms, but Ross and Mackenzie moved into the field of electrical technology with their takeover and electrification of the street railway systems of Winnipeg, Toronto, Montreal, Saint John, and Birmingham. From this base they undertook the promotion of a number of electrical power and electrical equipment firms. *ECB*, II, 21; *CMWT* (1898), 700, 887–88; *CMWT* (1912), 701, 972; *Montreal*, III, 22–23.
[30] *CCB*, I, 10; *ECB*, II, 25; *Prominent Men*, 99–102; *CMWT* (1912), 433–444.
[31] *CMWT* (1912), 472.
[32] *WWW* (VI & VII), 1107.
[33] *ECB*, II, 26.
[34] *CMWT* (1912), 577.
[35] *ECB*, II, 7; *CMWT* (1898), 787–88; *CMWT* (1912), 874–75; and Anne Wilkinson, *Lions In The Way* (Toronto, 1956).
[36] *CMWT* (1912), 21.
[37] *CMWT* (1912), 10.
[38] *ECB*, I, 107–108.

Senator Louis Forget began his career as a clerk in a Montreal wholesale house.[39]

The most dramatic examples of mobility for the native-born of humble origins and limited training were found in the rapidly expanding field of company service. The successes attained through this avenue were endless. James Redmond joined the Ames, Holden Shoe Company as a traveller and rose to the general managership of that firm and to the directorates of a half-dozen others, including the presidency of the Dominion Car & Foundry Company.[40] Charles Ballantyne entered the service of Sherwin Williams Paint Company while still a boy, and ultimately became a principal owner of the corporation.[41] The son of a farmer, Cyrus Birge entered the service first of the Great Western Railway then of the Canada Screw Company. He later led a consortium in purchasing the screw firm and finally became a principal in the great Steel Company of Canada consolidation.[42] But perhaps the most spectacular example of the use of this avenue of advancement was provided by Charles Hosmer, who, like Senator G. A. Cox, began his career as a telegraph operator, rose to the presidency of the company, retired with a fortune, and bought his way into some thirty-five major corporations.[43]

In large measure, however, social mobility and social continuity within the elite were a function of region. The incidence of second generation industrial families and the movement of prominent entrepreneurs from other fields into the manufacturing industries were particularly pronounced in the Montreal and Ottawa areas. This was reflected in the fact that nearly a third of the leading industrialists of the St. Lawrence region began their careers in firms belonging to close relatives. By contrast, those of the Lake Peninsula and the West demonstrated a far greater degree of social mobility. Farmers' sons, for example, comprised nearly a quarter of the elites of both latter regions, and the growing opportunities provided by the manufacturing sector were reflected in the surge of clergymen's, teachers' and even lawyers' sons into industrial vocations.

Yet, by 1910, one fact seems obvious — as the strength of the finance industrialist grew within the elite, and as that of the manufacturer industrialist waned, the opportunities for vertical social

---

[39] *ECB*, I, 38; *Montreal*, III, 112–19.
[40] *CMWT* (1912), 931.
[41] *CMWT* (1912), 56.
[42] *Industrial Canada*, December 1904; *ECB*, II, 31; *CMWT* (1912), 103.
[43] *ECB*, I, 13; *CMWT* (1898), 477; *CMWT* (1912), 548.

TABLE 13

OCCUPATION OF THE FATHERS OF THE
INDUSTRIAL ELITE OF 1910 BY REGION

	Maritimes	St. Lawrence	Lake Peninsula	West
Professional	7%	11%	20%	34%
Businessman	46	40	12	25
Manufacturer	26	33	31	8
Manager	14	6	12	8
Farmer	7	10	23	25
Craftsman	0	0	2	0
Labourer	0	0	0	0
Total	100	100	100	100
Total Cases	15	62	40	12

mobility became increasingly narrowed. New corporate structures and new technology could provide a certain element of fluidity, but at the level of ownership, the integration of the manufacturing sector into the business community as a whole was accompanied by horizontal rather than vertical mobility on the part of the personnel who moved into positions of command. The effects of this integration and of the rising status of the industrialist generally were reflected in the leadership which he provided in his nonbusiness activities. These will be viewed through his participation in political and religious institutions, and in the newly emerging elite clubs.

III

Like his predecessor of 1885, the industrialist of 1910 involved himself in the political process with a frequency matched only by members of the law fraternity in Canada, and one which was comparable to the level of political activity found among his American counterparts.[44] In all, nearly one-third of the members of the elite held political office at some time in their careers. Their activities, illustrated in Table 14, were scattered over the whole range of political endeavor. However, those who played the most important political roles — at the provincial and federal levels — were drawn overwhelmingly from the manufacturers as opposed to the financial industrialists. Outside the major metropolitan centers, most leading industrialists participated actively on the political scene, and

[44] C. Wright Mills, "The Business Elite: A Collective Portrait," *Journal of Economic History*, V (Supplement), 37.

TABLE 14

POLITICAL OFFICES HELD BY MEMBERS OF THE
INDUSTRIAL ELITE OF 1910 BY REGION [a]

Office	Region				
	Maritimes	St. Lawrence	Lake Peninsula	West	Total
Lt. Governor	1	—	1	—	2
Cabinet Minister	—	—	1	—	1
Senator	3	5	4	—	12
M.P.	4	10	6	—	20
M.E.C.	—	2	4	—	6
M.L.C.	—	1	—	1	2
M.L.A.	3	4	10	5	22
J.P.	—	1	1	1	3
Municipal	9	13	9	6	37
School Board	1	9	4	3	17
No. of individuals	11	27	22	12	72

[a] These include all offices held at any time before 1911.

even within these centers a significant number offered themselves
for public office.[45]

Perhaps the most striking political characteristic of the industrial
elite of 1910 was the degree of continuity in political attitudes.
This operated at two levels. Among those entrepreneurs found in
both the 1885 and 1910 elites, and among those members of the
1910 group who were sons of elite members of 1885, there was
virtually no change in political affiliation over the thirty-year
period.[46] There were, of course, instances of political conversion,
but these usually stemmed from a deep and bitter experience on
the part of the converts, such as several of the Irish Catholics in the
elite who left the Conservative Party over the Riel execution of
1885. Even more significant was the fact that, although the personnel of the industrial elite had largely changed, its regional political response remained relatively unaltered between 1885 and
1910. Industrialists in the Maritimes and the St. Lawrence regions
tended to be Conservatives; those in the Lake Peninsula were more
likely to be Liberals.

In religious activities, as in political, the participation of the industrial leaders of 1910 closely paralleled that of their counterparts

[45] For example, stockbroker E. B. Osler and tinware manufacturer A. E. Kemp represented Toronto East and Toronto West in Parliament throughout most of the first two
decades of the twentieth century (both were Conservatives), while their provincial Tory
counterpart, William McNaught, held Toronto North in the provincial assembly J. K.
Johnson, ed., *The Canadian Directory of Parliament 1867–1967* (Ottawa, 1967), 300, 451.
[46] The transportation entrepreneurs, such as the Allans, were a notable exception to
this generalization.

TABLE 15

POLITICAL AFFILIATION OF THE INDUSTRIAL ELITE

Affiliation:	1885 Elite	1910 Elite
Conservative	58%	54%
Liberal	40	44
Independent	1	2
Total	100	100
Total Cases	122	162

TABLE 16

POLITICAL AFFILIATION BY REGION, 1910

Affiliation	Maritimes	St. Lawrence	Lake Peninsula	West
Conservative	67%	57%	40%	57%
Liberal	29	40	60	38
Independent	4	3	—	5
Total	100	100	100	100
Total Cases	24	68	49	21

of 1885. All evidence would seem to indicate that, as a group, the former were churchmen who frequently participated at a high level of involvement in the life of their denominations. Nearly one in four was reported as having served in some denominational office, a proportion which rose to one in three in the Lake Peninsula. The proportion of officeholders was highest among the evangelicals, and nearly half the Methodist and Baptist industrialists served their denomination in some official capacity. There was, however, a subtle but significant shift in the nature of the offices held by the entrepreneurs of 1910 in comparison with their earlier counterparts. The latter had been mainly local church officers. But while many of the former continued to serve in these offices as well, they increasingly occupied the more prestigious provincial and national denominational offices as well as the trusteeships of their church colleges.[47] The commitment of most industrialists to their religious

[47] Thus, although Senator James Ross and Sir William MacKenzie continued to serve as ruling elders of their Presbyterian congregations, and the Hamilton steel manufacturer, Cyrus Birge, even retained the superintendency of a Methodist Sunday school, the more characteristic industrialist was the agricultural implements manufacturer Chester Massey who, in addition to his trusteeship of Metropolitan Church —Toronto's Methodist "Cathedral" — served both as president of Methodist Social Action and as a trustee of Victoria College. He shared this latter office with the tinware manufacturer, Albert Kemp, and the broker, A. E. Ames. A similar office was occupied at McMaster University by the Toronto paperbook manufacturer Samuel Moore, and by the Woodstock piano manufacturer, Dennis Karn — both leading Baptist laymen — while the founder of the Canadian General Electric

traditions appears to have been reflected as well in their philanthropic activities. The scattered and fragmentary evidence available on this subject seems to indicate that, while secular giving by industrialists was on the increase, most at least still contributed to both religious and secular causes. Their religious gifts were usually made to denominational colleges, while hospitals, secular colleges, and cultural activities were the recipients of most secular giving.

TABLE 17

RELIGIOUS OFFICES HELD BY LEADING INDUSTRIALISTS OF 1910

Office	Denomination						
	Pres.	Ang.	Meth.	Cath.	Bapt.	Cong.	Other
Local	10	4	6	3	—	1	2
Provincial	—	6	6	—	2	11	—
National	—	—	4	—	1	—	—
International	—	1	—	—	1	—	—
Church College	7	12	5	1	2	1	—
Interdenominational [a]	3	—	3	—	1	—	—
Total Offices	20	21	24	4	7	2	2
No. of Individuals	14	15	15	4	4	1	2
Proportion [b]	21%	28%	43%	13%	40%	25%	20%

[a] Includes Bible societies, Lord's Day Alliance.
[b] The proportion of the total adherents of the denomination in the industrial elite who held religious offices.

The rising status of the industrialist within the framework of the traditional denominational structure was but one reflection of the social changes wrought in the status and personnel of the industrial elite between 1880 and 1910 — changes which were the result of urbanization, of changes in the structure of industrial organization, and of the altering immigration patterns. Another institution which reflected this rising status and one which, as a class institution, competed with the more socially heterogeneous religious organizations was the elite club. In addition to the traditional club — seemingly drawn from the British coffee house — these new elite formations represented institutionalization into exclusive social organizations of a wide array of recreational activities, including riding, golfing, yachting, hunting, skiing, curling, fishing, polo, driv-

Company, Frederic Nicholls, served as a governor of Trinity College, and the Presbyterian financier, Robert Kilgour, served as governor of Knox College. See, on Senator James Ross, Montreal, III, 22–23, CMWT (1912), 972, Industrial Canada, December, 1904; on Sir William MacKenzie, ECB, II, 21, CMWT (1912), 701; on Cyrus Birge, ECB, II, 31, Industrial Canada, December, 1904; on Chester Massey, ECB, II, 10, Prominent Men, 326, CMWT (1912), 738, Merrill Denison, Harvest Triumphant: The Story of Massey-Harris (Toronto, 1948); on Albert Kemp, CMWT (1912), 607; on A. E. Ames, CMWT (1912), 21; on Samuel Moore, ECB, I, 84, CMWT (1912), 819; on Dennis Karn, CMWT (1912), 596; and on Robert Kilgour, CMWT (1912), 851–52.

ing, and tennis. The clubs were organized with surprising speed around the turn of the century. By 1910, virtually every community of 10,000 population – and several even smaller than this – had at least one of these organizations; most had several. Halifax, for example, had at least three; Toronto, fourteen, and Vancouver, five. Brantford, Peterborough, Sydney, and Calgary each also had at least one.

The overwhelming majority of the leading industrialists of every region, regardless of the size of the community in which they lived, held membership in one or more such clubs. The trend was most marked in Montreal, the community from which the movement appears to have emanated, but most industrialists from smaller communities usually held membership in the clubs of the nearest metropolis.[48] Indeed, increasingly, the true test of status was not one of whether an industrialist belonged to any major metropolitan clubs, but rather to which clubs he belonged and whether he belonged to elite clubs in several metropolitan centers.

While all industrialists generally participated in the club movement, merchants, financiers, and construction and transportation entrepreneurs among the elite were more likely to be found in club-rooms than were manufacturers. The religious dimension also played a considerable role in determining club membership. Presbyterians, Anglicans, and French Canadians within the elite, nearly 90 per cent of whom belonged to one or more elite organizations, participated most actively; Methodists, Baptists, and Irish

TABLE 18

SOCIAL ORGANIZATION MEMBERSHIPS OF INDUSTRIAL LEADERS OF 1910

Type of Club	Maritimes	St. Lawrence	Lake Peninsula	West
Fraternal Organizations Only	—	6%	6%	—
Local Elite Clubs Only	26%	40	23	50%
Fraternal & Elite Clubs	10	2	6	10
Elite Clubs in Several Centers	34	36	43	18
Fraternal & E.C. in Several Centers [a]	4	3	4	8
None	26	13	18	14
Total	100	100	100	100
Total Cases	27	105	55	28

[48] For example, Georgetown paper manufacturer John Barber and Orillia carriage-maker James Tudhope, were members of the Ontario and National clubs of Toronto; the Calgary brewer, Alexander Cross, was a member of both the Carleton Club of Winnipeg and the Union Club of Victoria, B.C. See *CMWT* (1912), 58; *CMWT* (1912), 1112; *WWW* (West), III, 171.

Catholics, were least involved in such organizations and appear to have been most committed to religious affairs. Such leading manufacturers and Methodist laymen as Chester Massey and Edward Gurney, for example, did not participate at all in the movement.[49]

Equally revealing was the pattern of extra-regional club membership. The variety of an entrepreneur's memberships usually reflected the scope of his business or ideological interests. For example, most Hamilton industrialists were members only of Hamilton or, occasionally, of Toronto clubs. By contrast, an interlocking corporate elite of Montreal and Toronto entrepreneurs generally held memberships in the Mount Royal and St. James clubs of Montreal, the Rideau of Ottawa, and the Toronto and York clubs of Toronto. The clubs of Senator James Ross, a leading member of this group, whose iron and steel, paper, and electrical interests covered eastern Canada, reveal the scope of the interests of the foremost industrialists. Senator Ross' memberships included the Mount Royal, the St. James, the Royal St. Lawrence Yacht, the Forest and Stream, the Montreal Curling, the Montreal Hunt, the Montreal Jockey, the Montreal Racquet, and the Royal Montreal Golf, of Montreal; the Rideau of Ottawa; the Manitoba of Winnipeg; the Toronto, the Royal Canadian Yacht, and the York of Toronto; the Union of Saint John; the Halifax and the Royal Cape Breton Yacht of Nova Scotia; the Manhattan of New York; and the Constitutional Club of Manchester.[50]

And in a sense, Ross, the Scottish engineer who achieved his first success in the Canadian railway construction industry, his second in electric railways, and his third in the steel and coal industry, epitomized what the industrial entrepreneur was in the process of becoming by 1910: a leader in industry, in state, in religion — a cosmopolitan figure of broad outreach and catholic interests.

IV

In conclusion, then, the characteristics which distinguished the industrial entrepreneur of 1910 from his counterpart in the 1880s were a reflection both of the changes which were restructuring the industrial life of Canada during the period, and of the demographic and social shifts which were steadily altering the fabric of Canadian society. Thus members of the later elite tended to be organization men or financiers rather than individuals who, through heroic per-

[49] *CMWT* (1912), 483, 738.
[50] *CMWT* (1912), 972.

sonal efforts, created major concerns. They tended, as well, to be found in those major cities in which the consolidation movements of the period had centered control of most manufacturing industry. And since industrial skills — in all but the newest technologies — were no longer a significant element in the industrial success of the individual entrepreneur, the industrialists of 1910 were far more likely to be lawyers, or high school graduates with some commercial training, than master machinists or journeyman clerks (although they still remained poorly educated compared to their American counterparts). Overwhelmingly they tended to be products of an urban or town environment; above all, they were members of an occupational group which was rapidly integrating into the business community as the new corporate organizations provided the opportunities for entrepreneurs to play significant roles in a variety of business activities.

The result was a narrowing of the high degree of social mobility which had marked the leaders in the 1885 elite. The industrialist of 1910 was much more likely to have been a product of upper middle class origins than was his predecessor. He typically found his way to success either through a two-generation diagonal form of social mobility, or through service in one of the established business institutions. Nonetheless, although success through the traditional industrial avenue — apprentice, journeyman, master — had become less common, new opportunities for advancement were opened as a result of the new corporate structures and of the new and more highly sophisticated technologies. In balance, upward mobility was less common within the later elite than it had been in that of 1880–1885, and in general it was a less spectacular rise.

In other respects the two elites demonstrated strong similarities. Members of both groups were characterized by their strong immigrant connections — in sharp contrast to their American counterparts — although the earlier group was distinguished by the presence (indeed, almost by the domination) of the immigrant industrialist, whereas the 1910 elite was dominated by the sons of British immigrants. As well, the relative positions of the several religious traditions remained constant throughout the period, although outside the St. Lawrence region they appear to have lost much of their ethnic associations.

Finally, the most significant continuity between 1880 and 1910 was the persistence of highly differentiated regional elites. Certainly the differences between the industrialists in any of the four regions defined in this study were generally more significant than the difference between the elites of 1885 and 1910. Nonetheless, the regional elites of 1910 were certainly more integrated into a national industrial system than their earlier counterparts had been. Thanks largely to the consolidation movements and to the federal industrial development policies, industrialists in all regions, and particularly those in the consolidation centers of Montreal, Toronto, and Halifax, sat together in the board rooms of most major industrial corporations and met to discuss their mutual problems in the lounges of those exclusive social organizations which more than anything else symbolized their growing stature within the national community.

By *Stephen Scheinberg*
ASSOCIATE PROFESSOR OF HISTORY
SIR GEORGE WILLIAMS UNIVERSITY

Invitation to Empire: Tariffs and American Economic Expansion in Canada

❡ *The growth of the United States' economic influence in twentieth-century Canada was intimately related to the continuation of the "National Policy" of protectionist tariffs. Professor Scheinberg argues that Canadians initially welcomed America's consciously expansionist thrust, and that they eventually became entangled in the problems of seeking rapid economic growth along with economic independence from both the older imperialism of Great Britain and the newer variety represented by the United States.*

The recent domination of the Canadian economy by American multinational firms has been thoroughly documented and widely debated.[1] Canadians have, however, been assured that their current situation resulted from geography, not policy, that American capital merely spilled over into Canada.[2] Above all, there was never any conscious attempt by the United States to establish an empire. "I can assure you," promised former U.S. ambassador Livingston Merchant in 1958, "that there is no sinister and no governmental design behind either our exports or our investments in Canada."[3] Then Undersecretary of State George Ball claimed there was no "conscious desire" to do so, while *Fortune* described the domination as "unplanned but nonetheless effective."[4] Finally, historian Hugh G. J. Aitken echoed these less scholarly declarations, contending that

Business History Review, Vol. XLVII, No. 2 (Summer, 1973). Copyright © The President and Fellows of Harvard College.

[1] See, for example: Report of the *Task Force on the Structure of Canadian Industry*, Privy Council Office (Ottawa, 1968); Walter Gordon, *A Choice for Canada* (Toronto, 1966); Kari Levitt, *Silent Surrender: The Multinational Corporation in Canada* (Toronto, 1970).

[2] Mira Wilkins, *The Emergence of Multinational Enterprise: American Business Abroad from the Colonial Era to 1914* (Cambridge, Mass., 1970), 67. Her chapter on Canada is titled "The Spillover into Canada."

[3] Livingston T. Merchant, "Behind the Headlines in Canadian-U.S. Relations," *U.S. Department of State Bulletin*, 38 (February 24, 1958), 297.

[4] "The Canadian Troubles of U.S. Business," *Fortune*, 56 (July, 1957), 139; George Ball, "Interdependence — The Basis of U.S.-Canada Relations," *U.S. Department of State Bulletin*, 50 (May 18, 1964), 770–74.

Canada 'is a satellite acquired almost by inadvertence, as an incident in the rise of the United States to industrial and military supremacy."[5] In other words, Canada may be an American economic colony, but this was never intended and should not be confused with the "wicked," that is conscious or planned, ventures of truly imperialist nations. This argument has provided one of the traditional *post hoc* defenses of empire. It is a variation on one of the familiar intellectual bulwarks of British expansion: the pieces just fell together, and one day there emerged an empire.[6]

The intent of this essay is not to reverse the verdict — to force Canadian-American economic history into a banana republic mold. The American economic conquest of Canada required no troops, no gunboats, no specific blueprint. Geographic proximity and cultural affinity eased the way for economic penetration, while Canadians welcomed and even gave positive encouragement to American capital. Yet the ease of American entry should not obscure the continuing active role of American businessmen and their government, persons who did not rely on geographic and cultural factors to secure Canada for American economic control.

From its very birth as a nation, the United States cast covetous eyes on the riches of Canada. Nor was this interest just a matter of grandiose visions or empty rhetoric. The "Empire for Liberty" was twice thwarted as it sought to use military means to extend its frontiers into Canada.[7] Sporadic movements for economic and political union continued through most of the nineteenth century. Disgruntled Montrealers issued their annexation manifesto in 1849, jingo politicians cried for new lands, while the transplanted Canadian Erastus Wiman and the transatlantic Professor Goldwin Smith of Cornell and Toronto labored to keep the dream alive. Professor Donald Warner, however, has rightly maintained that the serious movement for continental union played out its last act in the 1890s. Thereafter, annexation survived only in the chauvinistic oratory of shallow politicians.[8]

While the idea of political union died, the idea of Canada as part of the United States frontier survived. Settlers had always regarded the boundary lines as only a slight inconvenience, and as the frontier moved westward, settlement followed a serpentine trail that crossed and recrossed the border. Southern Ontario, states a noted historian

[5] Hugh G. J. Aitken, *American Capital and Canadian Resources* (Cambridge, Mass., 1961), 14.
[6] Robin W. Winks, ed., *British Imperialism* (New York, 1963), 6.
[7] Richard Van Alstyne, *The Rising American Empire* (Oxford, 1960), 55–60.
[8] Donald F. Warner, *The Idea of Continental Union* (Lexington, 1960), 241.

of Canadian business, was in the late 1870s and 1880s "a frontier society for Americans as well as Canadians." [9] It was not unique in that respect. The border regions constituted a shared frontier. Nothing as intangible as a surveyor's line or even the ties of nationalism barred the search for new opportunity.

For Americans at the end of the century, Canada was not a new frontier but a traditional ground for their interests. Perhaps it was that very familiarity which has led historians of American foreign economic policy to give little attention to Canada. Certainly it did not have the drama of the Spanish-American conflict or the intriguing quality of the markets of Asia and Latin America. The advance into Canada claims attention on other grounds. As an expanding American business system beset by periodic depression looked to expansion abroad as a means of economic salvation, Canada was not ignored. It became the largest field for American investment, a proving ground of the multinational firm, and a new frontier for American trade.

If some American businessmen were still overly enchanted with the prospects of more exotic fields to conquer, a writer for *World's Work* reminded them in 1901 that "trade-expansion like charity, begins at home." While "we are straining our eyes in the effort to see what we can do across the oceans," the writer continued, "we have expended little or no effort to bind closer to us the countries of the North American continent whose trade should be ours." [10] Even the Roman church, in the person of the ardently expansionist Archbishop John Ireland of Minnesota, called for this new means of expansion. "There will be no conquest, no war," Ireland proclaimed in 1903, "the hearts across the border are already beating with love for us, and commerce and agriculture are calling for espousals." [11]

As far as American businessmen of the late nineteenth century were concerned, the frontier to the north had reached the stage for the profitable input of their energies. After all, said the Canadian-born railway builder James J. Hill, "Canada is merely a portion of our own western country, cut off from us by accident." [12] There was work to be done there, and Henry M. Whitney, Boston industrialist and founder of Dominion Coal and Dominion Steel, made the American offer explicit: "The people of the United States would be glad to join with the people of Canada in developing this great

[9] William Kilbourn, *The Elements Combined: A History of the Steel Company of Canada* (Toronto, 1960), 35.
[10] J. D. Whelpley, "Our Relations With Canada," *World's Work*, II (July, 1901), 942.
[11] "The United States and Canada," *Current Literature*, XXXIV (April, 1903), 386–87.
[12] "Mr. Hill and Canadian Reciprocity," *Outlook*, 84 (November 24, 1906), 687–88.

area," said Whitney.[13] While there may be some temptation to understand such statements as only crass examples of imperial sentiment, they also represented the perpetuation of the nineteenth-century reality of a shared frontier.

It would have been surprising if those nineteenth-century movements for continental union had left no legacy. The crux of the matter is that continental union had been an available strategy for earlier groups on both sides of the border but had lost its appeal as new realities dictated new methods.

Even Professor Goldwin Smith recognized the folly of continued annexation efforts. In its most practical respects he declared (in 1907) that his dream had already been fulfilled: [14]

> The sporting worlds of the two countries are one. The summer resorts are in common. Canadians read the American magazines, American newspapers have a considerable circulation in Canada. American currency circulates everywhere but in Government offices. New York is the Canadian Stock Exchange. American investments in Canada are rapidly increasing.

Smith, although a strong continentalist, understood the change. It was no longer the case of the "sleepy Canada" Frederick Engels had seen in the 1880s as "ripe for annexation." [15] The moment for that strategy had passed, and most American leaders were content to forego the dubious pleasures of annexationist rhetoric for the tangible delights of economic substance.

The new United States strategy resulted from a number of forces. First, as Frank Underhill has rightly stressed, the Canadian National Policy, a protectionist program which took shape in the late 1870s, was a kind of declaration of economic independence.[16] However, some recent scholars have pointed out that there was another side to the National Policy. Prime Minister John A. Macdonald's policy included an implicit strategy for economic development through the use of foreign capital behind protective walls. There may be a certain irony here, for as Professor Michael Bliss has said, "the National Policy sowed many of the seeds of our pres-

[13] Henry M. Whitney, "Reciprocity With Canada," *Atlantic Monthly*, 106 (October, 1910), 464; Robert H. Montgomery, "Our Industrial Invasion of Canada," *World's Work*, V (January, 1903), 2978–98. Montgomery reported after a trip across Canada that "the industrial boundary of the United States runs in a waving line across the Continent well within Canadian territory." The journals of the day abound with statements of commercial interest in Canada.

[14] Goldwin Smith, "Canada, England, and the States," *The Living Age*, XXXV (April 27, 1907), 195–203.

[15] Frederick Engels to F. A. Sorge, September 10, 1888, in Karl Marx and Frederick Engels, *Letters to Americans* (New York, 1953), 203–204.

[16] Frank H. Underhill, *The Image of Confederation* (Toronto, 1964), 22.

ent problems with foreign ownership." [17] While Macdonald and his colleagues were aware of the implications of their strategy — in the short run — one should not forget that foreign economic domination was never perceived as a real threat during that period. American investment was stimulated, but not in amounts that would raise fears. Macdonald, of course, does not bear the responsibility for the failures of twentieth-century Canadian leaders to readjust to changed economic circumstances.

A second factor accounting for the American shift from annexationism was that the new strategy for Canada developed within the context of an important debate over empire, in the aftermath of the Spanish-American War. That debate, which focused on the Philippines, allowed policymakers to clarify American goals and to approach a new consensus on empire. The proponents of colonialism were satisfied with a few insular crumbs, Puerto Rico and the Philippines, but, far more important, the United States made its long-term commitment to the open door and informal empire as opposed to a colonial strategy.[18]

The application of the open door strategy to Canada took several forms. One factor of some importance to Canada was that the newly adopted American strategy found a convenient tactical ally in Great Britain. Britain's own interests in this period dictated a closer relation with the United States both in terms of traditional balance of power considerations and in terms of commercial concerns in China and Latin America. For Canada the most evident implication of this Anglo-American understanding was that British backing could not be counted on in disputes with the United States.[19] A second subtle but perhaps more significant implication of the American open door policy for Canada was that it necessarily closed the door to annexation. Finally, the open door would also operate in the future as one strategy for the economic penetration of Canada.

At the very time that some American producers looked to Canada as an outlet for their surplus production, other American businessmen looked to Canada in a more direct fashion, namely via the creation of branches. The multinational firm first arrived in Canada in the 1870s and 1880s. Among the early arrivals were Singer, Bell,

[17] Michael Bliss, "Canadianizing American Business: the Roots of the Branch Plant," in Ian Lumsden, ed., *Close to the 49th Parallel* (Toronto, 1970), 32.
[18] Thomas McCormick, "Commentary on the Anti-Imperialists and Twentieth Century American Foreign Policy," *Studies on the Left*, III (1962), 28–33, is the best synthesis of this debate.
[19] R. G. Neale, *Great Britain and United States Expansion: 1898–1900* (East Lansing, Mich., 1966).

Houston Electric (a forerunner of GE), and American Screw. By the end of the decade of the 1880s, one estimate places the number of American branch operations in Canada at close to fifty. These were branches of U.S.-based firms rather than companies which merely used American capital or employed American personnel.[20]

The branch plants were established for several reasons. At the most general level there was the expectation of profit. Locational advantage might have spurred on some of the firms even without the incentives provided by the National Policy, but other industries clearly required Canadian prodding. This took two important forms. First there was the protective tariff, which raised costs for some firms south of the border and led them to solve the problem by producing inside the Canadian market.[21] A second stimulus was the Canadian patent law. The Acts of 1872 and 1903 compelled American manufacturers to establish Canadian branches, license a Canadian manufacturer, or forego the Canadian market. The Act of 1872 required a patentee to establish a Canadian manufacturing facility within two years, if the invention continued to be imported after twelve months following the patent grant.[22] Thus the patent laws served as an important auxiliary of the National Policy. The organizers of Canadian Bell, for instance, began the manufacture of telephone equipment because they found that "Canadian patent laws required local manufacture."[23] A third incentive was the British Preference, which lured some manufacturers north with the promise of competing in the empire's broad markets. As "Canadian" producers, the American corporations were entitled to the imperial tariff preferences established in 1897. Finally, Canada's magnetism emanated not only from Ottawa and the federal government. Towns and cities competed with one another in their efforts to attract American investments. Free land, tax relief, and peculiar local features were the attractions held out to the American businessmen.[24]

[20] Wilkins, *Multinational Enterprise*, 45–46. Herbert Marshall, Frank A. Southand, Jr., Kenneth W. Taylor, *Canadian-American Industry* (New York, 1964), 12.

[21] Plymouth Cordage Co. seems to have come to Welland, Ontario for locational advantages. Treasurer's Report, 1908, Box H–2, Plymouth Cordage Co. mss., Baker Library, Boston, Mass. He stated that the Welland Plant enables "us to put Twine into the consuming districts as a [sic] less cost than we can from our Plymouth plant." Marshall, *et al.*, *Canadian-American Industry*, 199–202.

[22] An Act Respecting Patents of Invention, *Statutes of Canada, 1872*, 103–104.

[23] Wilkins, *Multinational Enterprise*, 51. Testimony of Francis J. Arend, Hearings, Senate Committee on Finance. Sen. Doc. 834, *Canadian Reciprocity*, I, 16–29, 1911. Arend, the treasurer and general manager of the leading manufacturer of cream separators, declared that the patent had driven his De Laval Separator Co. to establish in Canada.

[24] Edward Porritt, *The Revolt in Canada: Against the New Feudalism* (London, 1911), 109–130. Charles M. Pepper, *Report on Trade Conditions in Canada*, House Doc. No. 408, 59th Cong., 1st Sess., January 22, 1906, p. 1829.

These Canadian policies succeeded, perhaps too well. American investment in Canada in 1912 was over $400,000,000 and there were then an estimated 209 branch companies operating throughout the Dominion. While American investment was considerably less than the British, the character of investment differed considerably. The *Canadian Annual Review* of 1907 stated the difference succinctly: "Canada is to an ever increasing degree dependent upon British capital. It is not invested here with blare of cannon and the flare of sensational advertising; nor does it come largely in the form of personal investment in specific undertakings as does United States capital."[25] In other words, most British investment was in railroad and municipal bonds, portfolio investment, while the American capital was in raw materials and factories, direct investment conferring managerial control.

It was all very well for the large corporations with their surplus capital and their experience in branch management to establish new outposts in Canada, but smaller entrepreneurial enterprises could not easily follow the same route. These desires, for example, were articulated within the National Association of Manufacturers. Former NAM president David M. Parry, an Indiana carriage manufacturer, cogently presented their case in 1907. He observed that "the pressure to find a foreign vent for the surplus . . . [products of American industry] is becoming more intensified." If his fellow middle-western manufacturers were to compete, he declared, they required the opening up of the "principal foreign market in which they are interested, and that is the Canadian market. We need its raw materials and we can send it the finished product of our factories."[26] Both small and large manufacturers had an interest in disposing of what they termed an industrial surplus, but Canada's protectionist policies dictated varying responses within the American business community. The smaller manufacturers were forced to seek other means than the establishment of branches in order to crack the walls of Canadian protection.

THE RECIPROCITY DEBATE

An appropriate device was already available, the instrument of reciprocity. Protectionism had already served its major purpose for the United States; few American industries were "infant industries." High tariffs were becoming a nuisance for many American business-

---

[25] *Canadian Annual Review*, 1907, 47.
[26] D. M. Parry, "Reciprocity and the Middle West," *Annals*, 21 (May, 1907), 462-65.

men, but a nuisance that was difficult to eliminate.[27] Protection was still economically useful in some quarters, and ideologically and politically potent in others. Proposals for reciprocity, however, skirted these problems, and as free trade spokesman Edward Atkinson said, it served as the "common ground" for protectionist and free trader.[28] Reciprocity's broad utility was illuminated by John Ball Osborne, head of the State Department's Bureau of Foreign Trade. Each treaty, said Osborne, "will tie up one foreign country in the bonds of mutual interest." [29] It remained for that enthusiastic protectionist President William McKinley to confer general approval on the device. In September of 1901, on the eve of his assassination in Buffalo, the President confirmed the retreat from unyielding protectionism. "If perchance, some of our tariffs are no longer needed for revenue or to encourage and protect our industries at home," said the President, "why should they not be employed to extend and promote our markets abroad." [30] McKinley thus neatly straddled the protectionist sentiment with the pronounced intention of giving up only that which was no longer of real use.

Later that year an NAM-sponsored Reciprocity Convention met in Washington, under the chairmanship of NAM president Theodore Search. Staunch protectionists, rigid free traders, and moderates thrashed out the issues and finally arrived at a resolution which was virtually a recapitulation of McKinley's position. They asked Congress to continue "protection for the home market" but "to open up by reciprocity opportunities for increased foreign trade by special modifications of the tariff in special cases." [31] This ambiguous statement drew only three dissenting votes, but the aim of the NAM was to secure a consensus for reciprocity even at the cost of watering down the resolution.

The major problem for the reciprocity advocates was that in sacrificing a bit of protection, someone's ox had to be gored. That is, any agreement would require some concessions to Canadian interests. The desire of American producers for easy access to Canada's raw materials and trading markets caused them to favor lower

[27] Karl Marx, *Free Trade: A Speech Delivered Before the Democratic Club, Brussels, January 9, 1848,* translated by Florence Kelley Wischnewetzky with a preface by Frederick Engels (Boston, 1888), 10. Engels remarked that "protection ought to have done its task for America, and ought to be now becoming a nuisance."
[28] Quoted by Eugene Foss, *NAM Proceedings 1905,* 161.
[29] John Ball Osborne, "Expansion Through Reciprocity," *Atlantic Monthly,* 88 (December, 1901), 731.
[30] Quoted in *ibid.,* 721–22.
[31] *Proceedings of the National Reciprocity Convention* (Washington, D.C., November 19–20, 1901), 145–49.

American tariffs on Canada's natural products and Canadian reductions on manufactured goods. While this program appealed to some manufacturers, it did not have a similar allure for American farmers and lumbermen; consequently, politicians were most wary of entering this field. *The Chautauquan*, speaking for the farm and lumber interests, pointedly asked if the manufacturers' position meant "that not a single American manufacturer is to suffer in any degree from reciprocity?" This meant, they continued, "no reciprocity at all, for reciprocity in non-competitive products is a sham." [32]

Pressure for reciprocity with Canada continued through the first decade of the century, but so long as the manufacturers stood alone it was not a politically viable position. The balance of forces began to shift in 1907 when the American Newspaper Publishers Association commenced organized pressure for lower tariffs on newsprint. They had high hopes for tariff revision, as did many other Americans, but the Payne-Aldrich Act of 1909 disappointed them on two counts. First, the rates on newsprint were not lowered to the level incorporated in the House of Representative's Payne bill. The usual tariff logrolling had forced a congressional compromise with the paper makers. Second, the Payne-Aldrich Act included a policy of maximum tariff retaliation against those Canadian provinces which, through the use of export duties, tried to encourage the location of paper manufacturing within their bounds and to restrict the export of raw pulp.[33]

Faced with a serious threat to their most important raw material, the publishers pressed their view on President Taft. This combination has led L. Ethan Ellis, the most thorough investigator of the 1911 reciprocity agreement, to view its American side as mainly "the power of the press and of the executive office . . . closely linked to secure an end important to both." [34] On the other hand, Ronald Radosh, a recent student of the issue, has maintained that reciprocity was of more general interest to businessmen.[35] It was, but the addition of the publishers and their power created a coalition which was both economically anl politically potent. Now political leaders

[32] "Work of the Reciprocity Convention," *The Chautauquan*, XXXIV (January, 1902), 357–58.
[33] Testimony of John Norris, President, American Newspaper Publishers Association, *Canadian Reciprocity*, 219–224. The publishers insisted that they were seeking no favors, "we are asking to have an open door." Testimony of Don C. Seitz of the New York *World* in Hearings Before the Committee on Ways and Means, H. R., 61st Cong., 3rd. Sess., 1911, *Reciprocity with Canada*.
[34] L. Ethan Ellis, *Reciprocity 1911* (New Haven, Conn., 1939), 192.
[35] Ronald Radosh, "American Manufacturers, Canadian Reciprocity and the Origins of the Branch Factory System," *CAAS Bulletin*, III (Spring/Summer, 1967).

felt more pressure to accede to the manufacturers who had been raising their voices for over a decade. The power of the press would be united behind this proposition as on perhaps no previous economic measure in American history.[36]

While Taft's famous remark that Canada was at "the parting of the way" conveyed something of his outlook to the Canadian public, his most interesting observations were reserved for Theodore Roosevelt. He expressed his expectation that "the amount of Canadian products we would take would produce a current of business between Western Canada and the United States that would make Canada only an adjunct of the U.S. It would transfer all their important business to Chicago and New York, with their credits and everything else, and it would greatly increase the demand of Canada for our manufactures." [37] If Taft was correct, the fears of Canadian opponents of reciprocity were well founded.

Canada's most direct response to reciprocity was the defeat of Sir Wilfrid Laurier's government which had negotiated the agreement. Two major problems arise in the interpretation of the Canadian side of the reciprocity movement. First, why did the Laurier government agree to reciprocity after years of having adjusted its free trade principles to strong demands for the continuation of protection? Second, what factors account for the determined shift of Canadian business to the anti-Laurier forces, in response to a treaty which did not directly damage their interests?

Actually, Laurier and his ministers did not expect the American reciprocity proposal. It had been years since they had seriously considered reciprocity as one of their realistic options. The American invitation, however, represented a new opportunity for the old Liberal machine. They faced challenges from Nationalism in Quebec and from the growing pressure of the grain growers in the West. Reciprocity gave the Liberals an opportunity to reduce the pressure from the western farmers, and Laurier stressed this in his campaign. "The manufacturers must understand," he urged, "that there are men who are not as magnanimous as we are, and forces will be aroused which it will be impossible for me to control. . . . they are preparing for themselves a rod which will some day fall across their own shoulders." [38]

The attractiveness of the American proposal was that Canada

[36] Chicago *Tribune*, June 3, 1911, 1. Polling 10,000 newspapers in twenty-two states, they received 4,303 replies, of which 3,113 were definitely in favor.

[37] William Howard Taft to Theodore Roosevelt, January 10, 1911, in Henry F. Pringle, *The Life and Times of William Howard Taft*, II (New York, 1939), 588.

[38] Oscar D. Skelton, *Life and Letters of Sir Wilfrid Laurier* (New York, 1922), 379.

would give up so little for such great opportunities, or so it seemed. Laurier and his older colleagues could honor their more youthful ideological commitments with a small bow in the direction of free trade, and they seemingly could do so without damage to their acquired alliances in the business community.

Laurier, however, miscalculated. Canadian businessmen were frightened not by the treaty itself but by what they believed it foreshadowed. They saw reciprocity as the forerunner of future tariff reductions. Laurier lost their influential support and then lost the election.[39] One popular theory held that the great trusts were responsible and had financed the campaign of Laurier's opponent, Robert Laird Borden. The established American branches, claimed *The Independent*, "fear American competition if the tariff is reduced or removed. They have put their money into the election. They want the tariff wall and the higher the better."[40] It was a tempting explanation. Indeed during the campaign itself the Liberal Toronto *Globe* had attacked two of Borden's business supporters as agents of U.S. trusts. The *Globe* questioned if it was "pride in Canadian industrial independence and a 'high resolve' to keep Canada free from the domination of United States trusts that makes them cheer? . . . the International trusts they represent have stiff protective duties on both sides of the border. They fear these duties may be in danger by and bye."[41]

The evidence to support the fifth column hypothesis is not conclusive. Branch plant representatives were not unanimous in their sentiments. Spokesmen for Ford and International Harvester were staunch advocates of reciprocity. However, they represented the only manufacturing fields included in the treaty. On the other side, against reciprocity, the representatives of Quaker Oats and Sherwin-Williams were in evidence.[42] Robert Cuff has examined the interests of the Toronto Eighteen, a group of businessmen who jointly and publicly defected from the Liberals. Few of them, Cuff finds, had close connections with American corporations. He sees their imperial loyalties as a more important motivating factor in stimu-

[39] A Canadian, "Why Canada Rejected Reciprocity," *Yale Review*, I (January, 1921) 173–187; Clifford Sifton, "Reciprocity," *Annals*, 45 (June, 1913), 20–28. Sifton contended that "it was, and is, believed that reciprocity in natural products would lead to reciprocity in manufactures."
[40] "Reciprocity Defeated," *Independent*, 71 (September 28, 1911), 709–711.
[41] " 'Loyalists' and American Trusts," Toronto, *The Globe*, September 1, 1911, 6. The two Borden supporters were W. K. George of Standard Silver Co., one of the Toronto Eighteen, and W. K. McNaught of American Watch Co.
[42] "Manufacturer is for Reciprocity," Toronto, *The Globe*, August 14, 1911, 2; "Harvester Trust Plans to Grip Our Market," *Monetary Times*, 46 (March 11, 1911), 1016; *Canadian Annual Review*, 1911, 114.

lating the change. A United States Tariff Commission study of 1920 supports the hypothesis. It maintained that "American manufacturers with branch establishments in Canada were opposed to reciprocity because it promised to open the Canadian market to other American products."[43] Unfortunately the Commission did not offer evidence to substantiate this charge.

The case for the fifth column hypothesis rests, for the most part, on the furor with which the conservative spokesmen defended the branch plant against the threat of reciprocity. "American Capital Will Cease to Establish Branch Factories in Canada if Reciprocity Agreement is Approved," thundered one typical headline in *The Monetary Times*.[44] Another journal questioned whether branch factories would continue to come or indeed close down, "thereby bringing disaster in the places where they are situated."[45] Borden subscribed to that belief and used this argument against reciprocity to some effect in his campaign.

Canada's most respected economic historian, the late Harold Innis, once observed that "Canadian nationalism was systematically encouraged and exploited by American Capital. Canada moved from colony to nation to colony."[46] James Gray, a Canadian journalist, has also maintained that "in all the agitation for higher tariffs will be found the fine American hand of the United States industrialist who has opened a Canadian branch. The mere mention of the United States will send him rushing to Ottawa in tears . . . . Canadians are paying through the nose for the privilege of hearing American industrialists sing 'O Canada'."[47]

It may be the case that American branch plant industrialists exploited Canadian economic nationalism, but if so, they were not alone. Any advantage sought by branch plant representatives would also accrue to some Canadian capitalists. Thus the agents of the branch plants became good members and even leaders of the Canadian Manufacturers Association, not because there was an American plot to subvert it but because they viewed their interests in the same manner as did Canadian industrialists. Canadian nationalism may have been exploited for economic ends, but the

[43] Robert D. Cuff, "The Toronto Eighteen and the Election of 1911," *Ontario History*, LVII (December, 1965), 169–180; United States Tariff Commission, *Reciprocity With Canada: A Study of the Arrangement of 1911* (Washington, 1920), 76.

[44] "Americans Will Not Establish Branch Plants," *The Monetary Times*, 46 (March 4, 1911), 918–19.

[45] *Canadian Municipal Journal*, September 1, 1911, quoted in *Canadian Annual Review*, 1911, 257. On Borden see *ibid.*, 175.

[46] Harold Innis, "Great Britain, The United States and Canada," in *Essays in Economic History* (Toronto, 1956), 405.

[47] James H. Gray, "The Conquest of Canada," *The Nation*, 149 (August 5, 1959), 144–46.

exploiters came from both sides of the border. Indeed, one of the more interesting minor dramas of the 1911 reciprocity controversy was the spectacle of the Canadian-born railroader James J. Hill championing reciprocity in the United States and the American-born W. C. Van Horne of the Canadian Pacific leading the fight to "bust the damn thing." As Van Horne himself once candidly remarked, "patriotic sentiments have never in the history of the world stood long against the pocket book." [48]

DEVELOPMENTS AFTER LAURIER'S DEFEAT

The defeat of reciprocity temporarily thwarted the smaller manufacturers in the U.S. and strengthened the great corporations. Thus on the eve of World War I conditions favored the continuing development of American branch plants in Canada. Mackenzie King may have recognized these conditions as he prophetically confided to his diary: "The United States will rise out of the situation as the first power of the world. . . . The British Empire will be changed in complexion; the mother country will be crushed by the burden of the war." [49]

The Canadian economy was stimulated by the war's demands on both primary materials and secondary manufacturing. Canadian historian Donald Creighton has maintained that this gave Canadian manufacturers more control over their own national market since the British were "preoccupied." His judgment on the economy fits in nicely with the view of the war as a great Canadian national event, but this view is deficient in at least one important respect. In the period 1914–1919, twenty-seven major American firms established Canadian subsidiaries, compared to the twenty-two established in the years 1901–1913 and the twelve established between 1920 and 1924. Canada's national moment was also a moment to be cherished by American industry. The United States entered the war as a debtor nation and exited as the world's greatest creditor. She was also at war's end the primary source of foreign investment in Canada.[50]

[48] On the CMA see A. Morley Wickett, "Canada and the Preference," *Annals*, 45 (January, 1913), 29–46. The original statement of the "fifth column thesis" may be Edward Porritt, *The Revolt in Canada Against the New Feudalism* (London, 1911), 39. Walter Vaughan, *The Life and Work of Sir William Van Horne* (New York, 1920), 345.
[49] W. L. Mackenzie King, *Diary*, August 4, 1914, quoted in R. D. Cuff and J. L. Granatstein, "Canada and the Perils of Exemptionalism," *Queens Quarterly* (Winter, 1972).
[50] Donald Creighton, *Dominion of the North* (Toronto, 1962), 441. James W. Vaupel and Joan P. Curhan, *The Making of Multinational Enterprise: A Sourcebook of Tables Based on a Study of 187 Major U.S. Manufacturing Corporations* (Boston, 1969), 10. Cleona Lewis, *America's Stake in International Investments* (Washington, 1938), 351–375. F. H. Brown, J. O. Gibson, A. F. W. Plumptre, *War Finance in Canada* (Toronto, 1940).

The strengthened American position in Canada was proclaimed by American enterprise. In a 1919 report on Canada, the Guaranty Trust Co. issued a classic restatement of the expansionist thesis. "Even before the outbreak of the war," they explained, "we were reaching the point where as a nation there would be surplus funds available for investment." War had resulted in an increased surplus and "because we know Canada better than perhaps any other country, and because of the Dominion's great opportunities, our country ought to play a part in the development of the natural resources of Canada." [51] Through the 1920s American business continued to look to Canada for new opportunities.[52]

Increased American interest in Canada was encouraged by provincial premiers, including Quebec's Louis Alexandre Taschereau. The Premier's topic in his 1927 address to the Convention of Life Insurance Presidents was "The Challenge of Canada's New Frontiers." His plea for investment in Quebec's primary industries may have set the tone for his successors in subsequent years. You have, he promised his powerful audience, "an open field in Canada . . . not . . . handicapped in any way by legislation or taxation." Moreover, Quebec had more to offer them in electric power, "sane labor" and "sane laws that respect private property." [53] The audience could not have misunderstood Taschereau's message. Quebec and Canada were offered to the Americans as a new open door frontier for exploitation. Quebec's "sane labor" would not stand in their way, and investors could be assured that conservative governments would protect them.

EXPANSION OF
AMERICAN DIRECT INVESTMENT

The postwar period also afforded particularly lucrative opportunities for the expansion of American secondary manufacturing industries in Canada. Just as in the United States, the Canadian demand for consumer durables accelerated in the 1920s with consequent increased demands for electrical machinery and capital equipment. These were two fields in which Americans had clearly established their pre-eminence. Continuing Canadian hospitality,

---

[51] *Canada: Economic Position and Plans for Development*, (New York, 1919).

[52] Isaac F. Marcosson, "The Americans' Stake in Canada," *Saturday Evening Post*, 200 (March 17, 1928), 14–15. Scott Nearing, "The Economic Conquest of Canada," *The Nation*, 118 (April 16, 1924), 432–33.

[53] Louis Alexandre Taschereau, "The Challenge of Canada's New Frontiers," a speech delivered at the 21st Annual Convention of the Association of Life Insurance Presidents, December 8, 1927, pam., 7.

high tariffs, and imperial preference encouraged more American manufacturers to enter the Canadian market. The most significant of the new arrivals was the General Motors Co., which in 1919 bought out the Canadian McLaughlin interests to take its place alongside Ford on the Canadian scene.[54]

This upsurge of American investment, stimulated first by the war and then by the economic conditions of the 1920s, altered the nature of the political problems which American business confronted. Total American investment in Canada passed the $3,000,000,000 mark by the mid 1920s and continued to climb approximately $250,000,000 annually until the depression. While some smaller American manufacturers sounded an occasional call for reciprocity, the distinct interest of the large manufacturers and their branch plants was to perpetuate Canadian protectionism. In 1926, for instance, Canada reduced its auto tariff from 35 to 20 per cent. Henry Ford's personal response was to welcome the move, probably because his own thinking was still very much within the context of a narrow open door perspective. But the officials of Ford Canada set him right, and he reversed his position. Ford Canada relied on protection not only to safeguard its investment but to maintain its place in the imperial preference system. If drastic tariff reductions took place in Ottawa, imperial preferences would necessarily be reevaluated to prevent American inundation of imperial markets. Canadians were warned that if they wanted American capital to keep coming, manufacturers had to be assured that protection would continue to be observed.[55]

Yet the progress of the branch plants was not greeted with equal enthusiasm by all American economic planners. A debate that foreshadowed many of today's concerns began in Herbert Hoover's Commerce Department. Julius Klein, the Director of the Bureau of Foreign and Domestic Commerce, was concerned with the branch plant's impact on the export market, and, according to Professor Joseph Brandes, he evidently attempted to discourage direct investment. But Klein's assistant, Louis Domeratzky, resolved the issue in favor of the branch plant, and it was the latter who served as the principal Department expert on Canadian-American economic affairs. Domeratzky advised Hoover to disregard free trade over-

[54] D. H. Fullerton and H. A. Hampson, *Canadian Secondary Manufacturing Industry,* a study for the Royal Commission on Canada's Economic Prospects (Ottawa, 1957), 17–18. Marcosson, *"Americans' Stake."*
[55] Mira Wilkins and Frank Ernest Hill, *American Business Abroad: Ford On Six Continents* (Detroit, 1964), 131–32. Hugh L. Keenlyside and Gerald S. Brown, *Canada and the United States* (New York, 1952), 282. J. Courtland Elliott, "The Dilemma of Canadian Economic Nationalism," *The Annalist,* 27 (April 30, 1926), 611–12.

tures because most of the "American capital invested in Canadian industries is due to the Canadian Protective tariff policy." Given the fact, "free trade . . . would naturally detract from the value of the investment."[56] Understandably, there was very little encouragement given in this period to those who hoped for a general lowering of trade barriers between the two nations.

The American Smoot-Hawley tariff of 1930, which almost doubled the average duties, was in perfect harmony with this understanding of American economic interests. It was not, as some would have it, merely a short-sighted measure of narrow economic nationalism. Insofar as Canada was considered, the threat of a tariff war was dismissed, as was the possibility of an unfriendly government in Ottawa. Charles Bishop, writing for *Forbes*, put the matter bluntly: "Even if worst comes to worst, and a high protectionist government takes office at Ottawa, all that United States industry, following hundreds of examples, will need to do, is to establish more branch factories in Canada, get in on the protection to Canadian industry and incidentally, avail itself of the present or coming policies of preference to manufacturers in any part of the British Empire."[57] At last the cat was out of the bag. Canada could play the game with tariffs any way she pleased, but there was no real protection for her home-owned industries within the scope of the existing economic system. She could only choose the gravedigger, to be buried by American exports or by American branch plants.

Canada's new Prime Minister, R. B. Bennett, chose the latter. Tariff hikes and attachment to the preference system were at the base of his economic policy. Bennett was not only following the established Conservative Party logic, he was also hoping to stimulate a depressed economy. That time honored logic, however, operated in a different context than it had in Macdonald's day. The American branch plant was now a recognized threat to Canadian sovereignty. Yet the Canadian idea of nationhood was still being

[56] Louis Domeratzky to Herbert Hoover, March 10, 1925, in Herbert Hoover Papers (West Branch, Iowa), Hoover 1-I/47. Cf. Joseph Brandes, *Herbert Hoover and Economic Diplomacy* (Pittsburgh, 1962), 163–69. Brandes argues that Hoover and his aides discouraged direct investment. It is true that both Domeratzky and Julius Klein, the Director of the Bureau of Foreign and Domestic Commerce, were concerned about the impact of the branch plants on the export market. For his part, Domeratzky resolved the issue in favor of the branch plant on two main grounds.

First, he found that the key branch plant industries had actually shown a significant rise in exports since the war. Second, he believed that branch plants created healthier economies abroad and thus better markets for the export trade. "Our foreign industrial expansion," Domeratzky contended, "is an integral part of our economic development in the domestic field and is receiving its impetus primarily from our general industrial and financial progress." Louis Domeratzky, "American Industry Abroad," *Foreign Affairs*, VIII (July, 1930), 569–582.

[57] Charles Bishop, "Canadian Elections and U.S. Business," *Forbes*, XXVI (July 1, 1930), 44–45.

articulated in narrow political terms except by a small band of intellectuals clustered around the socialist Cooperative Commonwealth Federation.[58]

Both the Bennett and Roosevelt administrations looked to foreign trade as an important means of uplifting their depressed economies. Bennett, faced by the Smoot-Hawley tariff to the south, turned to the Commonwealth. The Ottawa Agreements of 1932 established new preferential duties within the Commonwealth. After Roosevelt's election, Canada began to review her trade relations with the United States. W. D. Herridge, Bennett's brother-in-law and ambassador to the United States, brought proposals for reduction of duties on some primary products to Washington. Undersecretary of State William Phillips welcomed this overture, forwarding the proposals to Roosevelt with his own advice that such positive action would serve as a stimulus to trade with Canada. Other sources close to the Roosevelt administration hoped for a trade agreement to help break down the Ottawa agreements.[59] No agreement was reached at this time. Within the State Department and through the administration a battle raged between economic nationalists and trade liberalizers. Bennett was not prepared to make the kind of concessions that might have appealed to both groups in the United States, and it remained for his Liberal successors to carry through negotiations.

Americans' objectives were well served by the two principal Canadians with whom they had to deal after 1935. The Deputy Minister for External Affairs, O. D. Skelton, was particularly continental in his emphasis. Vincent Massey, who served under him, believed that Skelton "had a strong and lasting suspicion of British policy and an unchanging coldness toward Great Britain . . . to put it bluntly . . . he was anti-British." [60] Massey might have added fullness to his characterization if he had also noted that Skelton believed that Canada's future was as part of North America. Mackenzie King, who came back to power in 1935, was of a similar mind. King amazed American Ambassador Warren Robbins with his de-

[58] Research Committee of the League for Social Reconstruction, *Social Planning for Canada* (Toronto, 1935), 53–56.

[59] William Phillips to Marvin H. McIntyre, April 26, 1933 in F. D. Roosevelt mss. (Hyde Park, N.Y.) P.S.F. Canada, Box 2. Phillips to Roosevelt, January 9, 1934 in *ibid.* Phillips to Roosevelt, October 31, 1934 in *ibid.* Memorandum on Canada prepared in Western European Affairs Division, Department of State to Phillips, April 26, 1933 in *ibid.* W. D. Herridge to Secretary of State for External Affairs, December 4, 1933 in Bennett mss (PAC, Ottawa), Series F, vol. 276, p. 184633.

[60] Vincent Massey, *What's Past is Prologue* (London, 1963), 135. Nancy H. Hooker, ed., *The Moffat Papers* (Cambridge, Mass., 1956). Moffat referred to Skelton as "North-American minded."

sire to convey his friendliness. Three hours after receiving birthday greetings from the Ambassador, King gratefully replied and sang the praises of U.S.-Canadian friendship as "the hope of the world." [61]

Robbins' successor, Norman Armour, was similarly touched by King's repeated attempts to express his regard for the United States. He reported having the following conversation with King on the subject of a new Canadian Ambassador to the U.S.: " 'You may think it a somewhat extraordinary suggestion to make,' he said, 'but if any of your people have anyone in mind that they think would fill the bill particularly well, I would be glad to have suggestions.' I laughingly passed this off by merely remarking that I felt sure we were perfectly safe in leaving that decision to him." [62] Skelton and King were not, of course, in any vulgar sense "sell outs." They were both men of integrity who felt comfortable among Americans, and while they recognized that Canadian and American interests would often diverge, they strongly believed that Canada had to reject an outmoded imperial outlook and resolve to live in North America. This new outlook would also facilitate further American efforts to integrate continental economic interests.

King had promised the Canadian electorate that reciprocity with the U.S. would be concluded, and when he took office he swiftly moved to accomplish that end. Phillips advised F.D.R. that two Canadian experts had arrived in Washington and helped to work out "a new set up which in our opinion is vastly more favourable to the United States than the one which was being considered with Mr. Bennett." [63] Tariff concessions were made to Canada on pulpwood, wood pulp, and newsprint, as well as cattle, cream, and seed potatoes. The United States gained reductions on autos and farm implements. The specifics of the 1935 agreements are, however, not as interesting as the premises on which they were based.

In a lengthy personal and confidential letter to Phillips, Norman Armour made the most penetrating assessment of American interests in Canada. Before the reciprocity treaty was approved, Armour had

[61] Warren D. Robbins to F. D. Roosevelt, December 18, 1934, F.D.R. mss, P.S.F. Canada, Box 2.

[62] Norman Armour to William Phillips, memorandum, October 25, 1935 in *ibid*. Moffat was highly favorable to King and characterized him as opposed to the Montreal and Orange Capitalists who relied on the British connection because a break would "speed the inevitable absorption of Canada by the United States." He also saw John D. Rockefeller, Jr., King's good friend, as a strong influence for close ties between the two nations. *Moffat Papers*, 341, 343.

[63] Richard V. Kottman, *Reciprocity and the North Atlantic Triangle, 1932–1938* (Ithaca, N.Y., 1968), 107. Phillips to Roosevelt, November 7, 1935, F.D.R. mss, P.S.F. Canada, Box 2.

a serious discussion with Skelton who threatened that "if we did not reach an agreement then it would probably mean that Canada would of necessity be forced back within the Empire." This would mean, said Armour, that Canada would become a "preserve for British exports and a part of a world wide British economic Empire." A trade agreement would prevent this, bring new opportunities to American exporters and bring "*Canada not only within our economic but our political orbit.*" [64] Here then was a golden opportunity for the United States to diminish the Ottawa Agreements, to use trade as a means to assure that Canada would be solidly a part of the American sphere of influence.

Armour did not only draw on Skelton for his inspirations. He perceived other advantages which were certainly not on Skelton's mind: [65]

> There is still time, while [the] Canadian economy is in a formative stage, to stifle the impetus away from highly competitive production to complimentary production. . . . Studies forwarded to the Department on the subject clearly reveal the possibility of developing some Canadian industries that do not seriously compete with our domestic production . . . The study and progressive development of such an economic policy would result in a larger and more stable market for American exports. Furthermore, the immensity of our national investment in Canada, estimated at $4,000,000,000 greater no doubt than our national investment in a number of our States put together, should argue the wisdom of the development of an increasingly close economic and political relationship with Canada which will protect it from the vicissitudes which might flow from the adventure of all British economic imperialism.

Several themes stand out in Armour's analysis of reciprocity. First, American trade and investment interests in Canada were regarded as threatened by British imperialism. Second, economic ties and political interests were not separately categorized but seen as interdependent. Third, and perhaps most interesting, the agreements were viewed as an opportunity to direct Canada's economic development on a path that would serve the interests of both American exporters and branch plant investors. A recent student of the 1935 agreement has termed the New Deal's reciprocity program "America's contribution to the restoration of international harmony and stability." [66] Perhaps so, but one must then understand what the American vision of harmony and stability was and Canada's place within it.

[64] Italics mine. Norman Armour to Phillips, October 22, 1935, in *ibid.*
[65] *Ibid.*
[66] Kottman, *Reciprocity*, 5.

CONCLUSION

World War II increased the opportunities for the United States in Canada. "Canadians find themselves in the curious position," said socialist Frank Scott, "that the more they contribute toward an overseas war effort, the more they push themselves toward financial dependence on the United States." [67] The Ogdensburg agreements of August 1940 began the process, establishing a joint board of defense for the continent. This was followed in April 1941 by the Hyde Park Declaration, in which the two nations agreed on specialization of munitions production. A Joint War Production Committee was established in October of that year to avoid unnecessary duplication. Further cooperation included Canadian assent to Article VII of lend-lease, which provided for post-war trade policy through "the elimination of all forms of discriminatory treatment in international commerce, and to the reduction of tariffs and other trade barriers." [68] It is clear that these wartime agreements followed much the same lines that Armour had stressed.

In the context of the war, Canadian compliance is not difficult to understand. King and Norman Robertson, Undersecretary of State for External Affairs, understood much of the process they were caught in. Robertson grieved over the American "assault on the preferential system," but believed that Canada was caught in an Anglo-American "squeeze play." [69] For his part, King feared that "with the United States so powerful and her investments becoming greater in Canada, we will have a great difficulty to hold our own against pressure from the United States." [70] Though they feared the loss of independence, the Canadian leaders were not prepared to change course drastically in wartime, if ever, and the war economy drew the two nations together through what one scholar terms "a process of economic fusion." [71] It was a process activated by men with a purpose, by men who planned for the future of a continental society.

The Americanization of the Canadian economy continued at an accelerated pace following the war, but the essential foundations had already been well established. America's expansionist thrust to

---

[67] Frank R. Scott, *Canada and the United States* (Boston, 1941), 70.
[68] James Eayrs, *In Defense of Canada* (Toronto, 1965), 20; R. Warren James, *Wartime Economic Co-operation* (Toronto, 1949), 29, 37–38.
[69] *Moffat Papers*, 355.
[70] C. P. Stacey, *Arms, Men and Governments: The War Policies of Canada 1939–1945* (Ottawa, 1970), 387.
[71] Quotation from James, *Wartime Co-operation*, 3. The United States note, which Canada concurred in, was virtually the same as Article VII.

the north was initially welcomed by almost all Canadians. It gained additional support within Canada as the branch plants added their voices to the chorus. Every empire has its unique features, and seldom has domination been achieved as easily as in the case of Canada. Yet Canada's willing submission to American capital did not obviate the need for purposeful action; perhaps it even served as a form of encouragement.

The English historian Seely once declared that the British Empire had been acquired in "a fit of absence of mind." [72] But contrary to Seely, modern empires are conscious creations, they require initiative from both business and government to create them, and vigilance and protection to maintain them. American practice in Canada confirms this judgment.

[72] Quoted in A. P. Thornton, *Doctrines of Imperialism* (New York, 1965), 23n.

By Patricia E. Roy

ASSISTANT PROFESSOR OF HISTORY

UNIVERSITY OF VICTORIA

Direct Management from Abroad: The Formative Years of the British Columbia Electric Railway

❡ *This is a case study of a London-directed firm that supplied transportation, gas, and electric power in British Columbia. Its history suggests that, in a young and rapidly developing economy, control of a company's activities by outsiders who are chiefly concerned with long-term investment prospects may be of greater benefit to all concerned than critics of absentee management are willing to admit.*

When Robert M. Horne-Payne, a London financier and the long-time chairman of the board of directors of the British Columbia Electric Railway Company died in 1929, the *Times* of London commented that one of his major enterprises, the B.C.E.R., was "a singular instance of a Canadian company controlled from London, yet run successfully and with profit." [1] While the claim was obviously exaggerated — the example of the Hudson's Bay Company immediately comes to mind — its sense was not completely in error. Most British investors in Canadian enterprises had allowed Canadians to manage their own businesses, sometimes with disastrous results. Horne-Payne himself had raised extensive funds for the Canadian Northern Railway, but two Canadians, William Mackenzie and Donald Mann, had controlled its unhappy destiny. The directors of the B.C.E.R., however, believed that British investors had "a very strong feeling" in favor of direct management through an English

Business History Review, Vol. XLVII, No. 2 (Summer, 1973). Copyright © The President and Fellows of Harvard College.

[1] *Times* (London), January 31, 1929, 14. See also F. W. Field, *Capital Investments in Canada* (Montreal, 1911), 22; Clark C. Spence, *British Investments and the American Mining Frontier* (Ithaca, N.Y., 1958), 92–93.

A leading example of an unsuccessful Canadian company controlled from London would be the Grand Trunk Railway, which had a London-based board but during the pre-war years allowed its manager, C. M. Hays, who resided in Canada, to dominate its policy. A. W. Currie, *The Grand Trunk Railway of Canada* (Toronto, 1957), 374. On the Canadian Northern Railway, see G. R. Stevens, *Canadian National Railways* (Toronto, 1962), II, 37–42. The author of Horne-Payne's obituary may have been thinking particularly of the British Empire Steel Company, which in 1920 amalgamated a number of coal, iron, steel, and shipping interests. By 1929 its British bondholders seemed likely to lose heavily on their investment. A major subsidiary of BESCO, Dominion Steel Corporation Limited, was in receivership.

board of directors.[2] Thus, Horne-Payne and his directors in London carefully controlled the affairs of their company, whose operations were 6,000 miles away in British Columbia.

Despite many problems of communication, and conflict between the directors and their managers in British Columbia, such management by a distant but well-informed board had much to commend it. In contrast to many similar enterprises, the B.C.E.R. was insulated from the spirit of boom which pervaded Canada between 1896 and 1913. Consequently, in forming developmental policies, its cautious directors could consider the company's long-term welfare as well as the immediate wants of British Columbia as conveyed to London by its managers.

Despite its cautious leadership, the B.C.E.R. did grow rapidly during these years. In April 1897, Horne-Payne had formed the B.C.E.R. by reorganizing and refinancing the small, financially troubled electric street railway companies of Vancouver, Victoria, and New Westminster, and the electric lighting companies of the first two cities. By 1913 he boasted of having created one of the largest electrical enterprises in the British Empire. It had a network of street railway lines in the cities and their suburbs, six electric interurban lines, gas companies, hydro-electric power facilities capable of generating more than 128,000 h.p., and an electrical distribution system throughout southwestern British Columbia. Moreover, the company was earning steady profits and was soundly financed with generous reserves.[3]

Caution was the core of Horne-Payne's policy. He rarely permitted his managers to develop new schemes in advance of actual need. And, no matter how desirable a new project might be, he would not permit the company to undertake additional expenditures unless he was certain of raising the necessary funds at reasonable rates. Such a policy of prudent attention to the financial situation required the board to exercise close control over management. The benefits of such a policy more than compensated for any conflict between the board in London and its managers, who were regularly subjected to local demands for new and improved services.

---

[2] G. P. Norton to J. Buntzen, March 16, 1904, British Columbia Electric Railway Papers, Box 73. (All manuscript sources cited are from these papers, which are located in the Library of the University of British Columbia, Vancouver.)

While the British Columbia public occasionally complained about absentee ownership and management, the question of "foreign" ownership did not arise. Although British Columbia had been a province of Canada since 1871, remnants of the colonial mentality persisted. Many British Columbians, even those born in Canada, regarded Britain as the "mother country."

[3] In 1913 the company earned a net profit of £381,424 and had a total reserve of £924,346. B.C.E.R., *Annual Report*, 1913.

While the manager was often an advocate of the wants of British Columbia, he never seriously questioned the fact that his primary loyalty was to the board of directors. He knew he was their servant and not a policy maker. His task was clearly limited to the interpretation of the needs of British Columbia to the board and to the execution of the board's decisions. During the first few years of the company's existence, he was not permitted to act on any but the most minor of day-to-day matters without consulting the board. As the company developed and prospered, and as London-trained men took over as managers, the board gave the manager greater freedom in routine affairs but never gave him authority to make policy himself.

The board's idea that the manager should be its servant quickly became evident. When the company was first organized, F. S. Barnard, a prominent local businessman and politician who had controlled the B.C.E.R.'s immediate predecessor, was named managing director. Soon after incorporating the Vancouver Power Company to develop water power resources and spending money on capital account without the sanction of the board, Barnard "arranged to resign" his managerial post.[4] Because the board believed the manager should do little more than supervise the operations of the company, they proposed to designate his successor, Johannes Buntzen, "General Superintendent." Buntzen rejected this title which, he argued, implied an expert electrician. Reluctantly, the board named him "General Manager" but gave him no more authority than they would have given a "superintendent."[5]

To strengthen their control over management, the directors trained young men with close connections with the English side of the business as future managers. When poor health forced Buntzen to retire in 1905, the first of these young men was ready. R. H. Sperling probably got his first job with the B.C.E.R. through his father, a director of the B.C.E.R. and a member of the stockbroking firm which initially floated the company. The board, however, had not sacrificed the safety of the investment to practice nepotism. Sperling, an electrical engineer by profession, rose through the company's ranks on his own merits. He remained as general manager throughout the years of the company's most rapid growth, retiring in the spring of 1914 because of uncertain health and the desire of Horne-Payne to have an advisor in London with "a complete up-to-date knowledge" of the company's affairs in British

[4] Board of Directors, Minutes, April 12, 1898, Box 687. Barnard remained a nominal member of the board of directors until 1904.
[5] Buntzen to H. Williams, January 27, 1898, General Letter Book, #1. (Hereafter GLB.)

Columbia.[6] Meanwhile, the company had continued to train potential managers by having them serve apprenticeships as Secretaries of the company in London. As the main function of the Secretary was to transmit information from British Columbia to London and *vice versa*, the incumbent was in an excellent position to gain an overall view of the company and to be observed by the board.

Horne-Payne required his managers to keep him well-informed of the day-to-day details of the company's operations. He read every letter received from Vancouver and spent some time each morning on the B.C.E.R.'s affairs before attending to his other business interests.[7] Communications on matters of finance and appropriations were usually carried out by letter, whereas operating results were cabled to London. This routine was as indicative of the board's conception of the role of its manager as it was of its desire to have current information to assist it in raising funds. When Buntzen complained that he could not plan efficiently without full knowledge of the amount of funds available, the board agreed to use the cable more frequently. This, of course, increased their control over routine decisions.

The system was not perfect. In 1900, for example, unforeseen circumstances forced Buntzen to ask the board for a temporary loan of $50,000 to pay his creditors. He had, in fact, knowingly overspent in the short run by rushing two authorized projects to completion. He had anticipated that a new preference issue would provide the necessary capital, but he did not have any official word of the new issue.

Nevertheless, Horne-Payne did not chastise Buntzen. After analyzing their correspondence over the previous nine months, he concluded that neither Buntzen nor himself could be blamed for an error in calculations. The mistake, he declared, was "due to the great distance between London and Vancouver which makes it impossible to keep properly in touch, and to keep track of the capital expenditure of unforeseen discription [*sic*] which occurs from time to time." To prevent a recurrence of the problem, he suggested a complicated system for revising estimates on the basis of actual costs and previous experience. Buntzen replied it was impossible to estimate capital needs in this way. Prices fluctuated, parts of

<hr>

[6] R. M. Horne-Payne to R. H. Sperling, May 5, 1914, Box 68. The managers of the B.C.E.R. played an active role in civic life. Although Buntzen and Sperling left British Columbia after retiring as managers, they did not act merely as sojourners while in the province. Compare Rex A. Lucas, *Minetown, Milltown, Railtown* (Toronto, 1971), 153–54.
[7] Horne-Payne to Buntzen, November 21, 1902, Box 73. Horne-Payne was clearly the dominant member of the board, although his directors did participate in policy making and undertook visits to British Columbia.

the plant were wearing out, and civic decisions to pave streets could lead to unexpected expenses in the relaying of tracks. He proposed a monthly comparative trial balance as a means of keeping the board informed of his financial situation, and he urged that he be given a great deal of discretionary power. The board regularly reaffirmed its faith in Buntzen and his staff but would not grant him the power he desired. Nor is there any record of the directors replying to his suggestion of a comparative trial balance. Eventually, the board tried to solve the bookkeeping problem by sending an English accountant to Vancouver to bring the London and local auditors more closely in touch. New forms were devised and the board went to the additional expense of cabling the monthly financial memorandum, but the problem was never completely overcome. Fortunately, the basically sound financial position of the company permitted it to borrow short-term funds on favorable terms to meet occasional emergencies. And, the conservative expansion policy of the company meant that emergencies were rare and never involved large sums.[8]

In another attempt to overcome the problem of distance, Buntzen asked the directors to appoint a local board of directors to assist him in recommending new programs and to advise him on matters which could not be explained completely by letter or cable or which had to be decided quickly. Realizing that the board opposed any scheme which would reduce its authority, Buntzen repeated his request but did not press the issue. In 1905, however, the board opened a local register for the convenience of British Columbia shareholders. In order to have share certificates and other documents signed without transmitting them to London, the board established a local advisory committee which also had an important public relations function. Its members — F. S. Barnard, R. G. Tatlow, M.L.A. for Vancouver and provincial Minister of Finance, and W. H. Keary, Mayor of New Westminster — were expected to use their personal influence on the company's behalf and to give advice when asked. The advisory committee met about once a month but was not responsible in any way for the management of the company.[9] In 1911, the board abolished the committee. There had been public criticism of possible conflict of interest involving Tatlow and Keary and, its immediate purpose, the signing of share certificates,

[8] Horne-Payne to Buntzen, October 23, 1900; Buntzen to Horne-Payne, December 11, 1900, Letters from the General Manager. (Hereafter LFGM.)
[9] Buntzen to Francis Hope, September 14, 1898, General Manager's Letter Book (hereafter GMLB); Buntzen to Hope, November 13, 1899, LFGM; Buntzen to Norton, February 5, 1904, Box 73; Buntzen to F. S. Barnard, May 31, 1905, LFGM; Buntzen to Barnard, June 5, 1905, LFGM; Local Advisory Committee, Minute Book.

had declined in importance. Problems of English income taxes, losses on currency exchange, and the presence of more alluring investment prospects at home made B.C.E.R. issues unattractive to local investors.

Horne-Payne had been reluctant to experiment with the requests of both Buntzen and Sperling that he cultivate good will by setting aside a portion of new share issues for purchase in British Columbia. While the board was anxious to promote good will, it feared that the circulation of financial information designed to appeal to potential investors would cause agitation among customers and politicians who thought the B.C.E.R. was charging too much for its services. For the same reason, the board occasionally accepted the advice of its manager and paid a slightly lower dividend than might have been justified by profits. They refused, however, to reduce the dividend to a rate which would interfere with their ability to raise new capital.

Concern for financial stability underlay the board's policies. Because of their dependence on the capital markets, they knew they did not have access to an unlimited or an assured supply of funds. They were reluctant to spend capital in anticipation of successful issues; they refused, except in emergencies, to raise funds other than by the sale of shares and long term debentures; and they were usually unwilling to expand their operations without convincing evidence of immediate returns. This policy quickly earned the B.C.E.R. a reputation as a "safe" investment which paid regular, if modest, dividends and thus assisted it in raising funds at comparatively cheap rates. To insure that he would have cheap money, Horne-Payne deliberately delayed issues whenever conditions were unfavorable. Unfortunately, periods of tight money in London and rapid growth in British Columbia sometimes coincided. The subsequent conflict between the board and management illustrates some of the problems of control from abroad. It also demonstrates how the company, by considering the financial situation first and the wants of its customers second, was spared the financial tragedies which beset many locally controlled public utility companies.[10]

---

[10] Between 1897 and 1913 the B.C.E.R. raised over £9,000,000. About 60 per cent of this was obtained by the sale of debentures of which 80 per cent were issued at 4¼ per cent. Most Canadian industrial bond issues had to pay between 4.94 and 5.33 per cent. [Jacob Viner, *Canada's Balance of International Indebtedness, 1900–1913* (Cambridge, Mass., 1924), 98.] The remainder of the B.C.E.R.'s capital was raised by the issue of shares. These paid a maximum dividend of 8 per cent — and that on Deferred Ordinary Stock, which had the least preference in the time of adversity — whereas other Canadian tramway and lighting companies were paying from 6 to 12 per cent in dividends.

One reason for the company's ability to raise money cheaply was its reputation for safety. The directors had deliberately sought to make B.C.E.R. preference shares eligible

Between 1898 and 1900 Buntzen repeatedly warned the directors of the inadequacies of the plant inherited from its predecessors and the danger of competition. Moreover, as a result of boom conditions stimulated locally by the Klondike gold rush, the demand for the company's services exceeded its capacity. The board would do no more than reallocate appropriations from the street railway to the more pressing needs of the lighting system. Although the gross profit for 1899 was £30,189, the Board refused to appropriate additional funds or to pay more than a 4 per cent dividend on ordinary shares. The surplus was transferred to reserves, another indication of a careful husbanding of the company's financial resources. Buntzen finally demanded a clear-cut policy statement: "Are we to follow up the growth of British Columbia cities and extend our lighting system as the city extends and run new car services where such service, in our judgment here, is required? Or will the Company be satisfied to do the business they are now doing and leave it to others to take up the new business with the knowledge that any new company coming in will not be satisfied with such new ground only, but will also cut into our present business as soon as they have a firm footing in the City." [11] The board was willing to risk the possibility of competition. They informed Buntzen that until a new preference issue could be successfully floated, "no matter how much or how profitable business may be offered you, if it involves further capital outlay it must be refused . . . [because] . . . the Board prefer running all risks of competition . . . to the risks they would run by borrowing money on capital account repayable at fixed dates." Privately, Horne-Payne advised that "floating debt is the great enemy of Joint Stock enterprise and has brought more good concerns to bankruptcy than any other cause." [12] Buntzen had a clear-cut policy statement; the board would not risk financial distress, they would follow a prudent course, and Buntzen would have to do likewise. The directors, isolated from the public their company served, could afford to ignore pressure for improved service until the financial picture was more favorable. The risk, however, was not that great. They knew that any potential rival, private or public, would also have great difficulty in raising funds.

as trust investments under English law. An examination of the records of shareholdings in the Company Registry Office in London suggests that most investors in the B.C.E.R. looked upon it as a long-term investment. Of the approximately 5,000 individual shareholders in 1912, about half were women and most of the males were "gentlemen" or professional men. Most held no more than a few hundred shares and only about 15 per cent bought or sold any shares during the year.

[11] Buntzen to Hope, February 24, 1900, GLB, #5.

[12] Hope to Buntzen, March 20, 1900, Box 688; Horne-Payne to Buntzen, March 21, 1900, Box 73.

During most of 1903 and part of 1904 the London capital market was again difficult. The B.C.E.R. did not make a planned issue of £50,000 preference shares and had to resort to borrowing £100,000 on the basis of two year promissory notes bearing 6 per cent interest. In spite of his "splendid returns," the directors ordered Buntzen to cut down on already authorized projects and future plans. He immediately postponed a one-and-a-half-mile extension of the street railway through a rapidly developing residential area of Vancouver to the cemetery and curtailed plans for new rolling stock and machinery. The opportunity to make a relatively quick return on additional investment and to meet local complaints of unsatisfactory service was temporarily set aside in order to safeguard the company's financial stability.[13]

Buntzen was thoroughly frustrated by the company's inability to go ahead with such promising plans. He complained that "the Board without local knowledge, and without being in touch with British Columbia people, cannot possibly form an independent opinion of our business here." He hinted that if the board did not have full trust in him, they should replace him. He repeated an earlier request for the establishment of a local advisory committee and asked that one of the directors visit British Columbia.[14] The board could only counsel patience. They agreed that essential works must continue, they recognized that the company had to keep pace with the growth of the cities, but, they admonished, "if money cannot be got at a given moment, and just at a time when demands are somewhat larger than usual, the Directors feel that a little caution on their part is not out of place." Fortunately, the B.C.E.R. was able to raise some funds among its friends and larger shareholders, and, during 1904, it succeeded in issuing £140,000 worth of various categories of stock.[15]

Money was becoming much easier to obtain as British trade revived after the post-Boer War depression. During the following nine years, the B.C.E.R. issued almost £6,500,000 worth of stock and debentures, frequently at a premium.[16] Nevertheless, Horne-Payne continued to be cautious. Whenever he sensed possible difficulty in raising new capital, he warned his manager to husband

[13] Hope to Buntzen, January 13, 1904, Box 691; Hope to Buntzen, February 12, 1904, Box 691; Norton to Buntzen, March 16, 1904, Box 73; B.C.E.R., *Annual Reports*, 1904 and 1905.
[14] Buntzen to Hope, February 3, 1904, LFGM; Buntzen to Norton, February 6, 1904, Box 73; Norton to Buntzen, March 16, 1904, Box 73.
[15] Hope to Buntzen, March 5, 1904, Box 691; Hope to Buntzen, April 23, 1904, Box 691; Report of Norton and Slade, auditors, July 9, 1917, Box 89.
[16] Report of Norton and Slade.

cash resources, to postpone all non-essential projects, and to work on only one major development at a time. He also insisted that he be kept well informed of capital expenditures as far in advance "as possible." [17] Between 1905 and 1913 the B.C.E.R. rarely suffered serious financial stringencies. The occasional periods when the management was in straitened circumstances passed quickly. Generally, the company had such a sound reputation that it was able to raise money even when, as in 1912, Canadian municipalities were unable to do so. The healthy financial situation also improved the relationship between the board and management, a relationship which was strengthened by family ties (the Sperling family were major shareholders), by regular visits of board members, and especially by the fact that the B.C.E.R. was earning sufficient revenue to pay increased dividends and justify new expenditures for street railway expansion and hydro-electric power development.

Occasionally, favorable money markets, handsome profits, and increasing reserves lulled the directors into lapsing from their normal caution. Such lapses reinforced the need for effective communication and close control of the management. Mistakes could be costly, as the construction of the twenty-mile-long interurban from downtown Victoria through the rural Saanich peninsula showed. After approving a preliminary survey and the seeking of land bonuses from property owners along the route, the directors had second thoughts about the wisdom of building it. "We trust," the board wrote Sperling, "you have done nothing to commit us to the immediate construction of this line." [18] When the board claimed that it had always discouraged the construction of this line, Sperling quoted specific letters and cables authorizing him to prepare for it. There had been a breakdown in communication. The board had never expressed any great enthusiasm for the project, but it had not taken any positive steps to discourage it. More significantly, two directors who visited Victoria in the summer of 1909 had not denied the statement of a Victoria journalist that the Saanich line was part of an agreement with the city. The scheme could not be abandoned. When rumors circulated in Victoria that the line might not be built, local civic bodies objected. Premier Richard McBride, a good friend of Horne-Payne, warned that failing to build the line would have

[17] B. Binder to Sperling, December 1, 1906, Box 694; B.C.E.R. (London) to Sperling, November 15, 1907, LFGM; George Kidd to Sperling, November 18, 1908, Box 698; Kidd to Sperling, January 7, 1909, Box 29A–393; Kidd to Sperling, June 26, 1909, Box 700.
[18] Kidd to Sperling, March 29, 1910, Box 549; Kidd to Sperling, July 7, 1910, Box 549. I have described the relationship between the Saanich line and the city of Victoria in "The Fine Arts of Lobbying and Persuading: The Case of the B.C. Electric Railway, 1897–1917," in David S. Macmillan, ed., *Canadian Business History* (Toronto, 1972), 252–53.

"a most disastrous effect on the standing of your corporation in British Columbia." Subsequently, the board, unwilling to risk antagonizing the provincial government on which it depended for many favors, approved the construction of the Saanich interurban.[19]

This line never earned a profit and was abandoned eleven years after its completion. It was an expensive reminder of the many difficulties in operating a company some 6,000 miles away, and it forced the board to reiterate their traditional idea that the manager was simply their servant. After declaring that they had not been committed to the Saanich line, they advised Sperling that "in order to avoid any misunderstandings in the future will you please be good enough to understand that when any information, proposal or casual reference is made by you in a Weekly News Letter or by other means to do anything requiring the sanction or views of the directors, it must not be assumed that the Board's approval has been conveyed unless a specific reply is received by you." [20] This, coincidentally, was one of the last letters written by Kidd as Secretary; a short time later, he moved to Vancouver as assistant general manager, thus strengthening the link between the head office in London and the scene of operations in British Columbia.

The directors' failure to clarify their position in Victoria is exceptional in light of their shrewd examination of railway projects on the Lower Mainland. Before deciding to extend existing lines or to build new ones there, they carefully considered their overall financial position, traffic opportunities, possibilities of bonuses or concessions, and the effect on their overall strategy of improving the status of their franchises.

Within the city of Vancouver itself, the company received many requests for extensions to existing lines. A few of these extensions involved such comparatively minor expenditures that management officials authorized their construction, which was paid for from general appropriations for street railway improvements. In some cases, these officials could see no merit in a particular extension and did not bother to refer it to the board unless, for local political reasons, they wished the board to bear the odium of rejecting it. Most requests for extensions, however, were referred to London for the board's consideration and decision. In 1905, for example, Sperling recommended the expenditure of approximately $12,000 to extend the Harris Street line a mile in order to exploit the traffic

[19] Kidd to Sperling, January 4, 1911, Box 549; Sperling to Kidd, January 25, 1911, Box 549; Sperling to Secretary (London), April 8, 1911, LFGM; Richard McBride to Horne-Payne, January 27, 1911, Box 40–629.
[20] Kidd to Sperling, February 25, 1911, Box 47B–844.

of a well developed area and to relieve over-crowding on other lines. The board accepted his recommendation but suggested that he not promise to build the line until the city gave the company favorable terms on the street lighting contract, then being revised.[21]

In offering advice on strategy, the board was able to use its extensive knowledge of the experience of other street railway companies and was not dazzled by offers of land or cash bonuses. In the spring of 1910, two property owners offered to arrange to have land owners pay the cost of constructing a short line on their street. Sperling was enthusiastic about the idea. Not only would the company save on capital expenditure, but the new line would improve service to Kitsilano Beach and to a rapidly growing residential area. The board, however, rejected the scheme. They were not satisfied that it was the best way of meeting traffic requirements; they preferred to develop suburban areas where they had long-term franchises and, they reminded Sperling, "many Electric Railways have been ruined by the multiplication of lines within a small city area. This was notably the case in Minneapolis."[22]

The board's attitude to new lines was not wholly a negative one. Indeed, the decision to build the company's major railway project, the sixty-five-mile-long Fraser Valley branch from New Westminster to Chilliwack, was the result of the initiative of a board member. The B.C.E.R. had studied the traffic potential of the Fraser Valley over a relatively long period of time. However, it had ignored the requests of residents of the southern side of the valley for a railway because there was insufficient traffic in sight to justify one even if the B.C.E.R. had been in a position to raise the necessary funds.

Just before he retired as general manager in the summer of 1905, Buntzen told the Chilliwack *Progress* that he hoped to present the directors with "the question of future tramway extension from Steveston [at the mouth of the river] up the river and possibly from New Westminster south if sufficient inducements should be offered. By being on the board of directors and at the same time in close touch with conditions here through the general manager, Mr. Sperling, the directors will be more thoroughly acquainted with the various needs for improvements and extensions to the system than was possible by the most lengthy correspondence."[23] When he re-

---

[21] Sperling to Buntzen, November 24, 1905, Box 2–18; Buntzen to Sperling, December 13, 1905, Box 2–18.

[22] Sperling to Kidd, April 12, 1910, LFGM; Kidd to Sperling, May 4, 1910, Box 41A–647.

[23] Chilliwack *Progress*, July 19, 1905.

turned to British Columbia a year later, Buntzen observed the marked growth of the eastern Fraser Valley. The idea of building a line from New Westminster east to Chilliwack through the best agricultural districts of the valley strongly appealed to him, though he had not discussed it in London.[24] His enthusiasm for the potential traffic was supported by the business the B.C.E.R. was already securing through its connection with a river steamer. It also seemed likely that if the B.C.E.R. acted quickly, the municipalities would offer generous light, power, and railway franchises.

Early in 1907, when the board definitely decided to build the Fraser Valley branch, the company's finances were in excellent condition. Nevertheless, when Horne-Payne anticipated difficulty in raising additional funds because of the world-wide financial depression, the board instructed Sperling to concentrate his resources on the Fraser Valley line.[25] The importance of the Fraser Valley branch was also emphasized by the close supervision the board exercised over its construction. When final surveys indicated that construction costs would be higher and land bonuses less generous than anticipated, the board advised Sperling to delay making a final choice of route until he had exhausted all possibilities of land bonuses and until one of the board members had had an opportunity to examine the three routes surveyed.[26] While the line was being built, several directors, including Buntzen, made extensive visits to British Columbia.

After the Fraser Valley line was completed in October 1910, the board insisted that the traffic potential be fully exploited before it would even countenance as much as a survey for branches from it. In 1912, however, Sperling recommended that the company extend the line six miles eastward to Rosedale, a fertile and developed agricultural area, in order to compete with the Canadian Northern Railway, which was building through the district. The board rejected the proposal, explaining that a price war might develop between the two railways and force the B.C.E.R. to reduce its rates along the whole of the line.[27] A more telling reason was the serious

[24] Buntzen to Binder, June 17, 1906, Box 665.
[25] Binder to Sperling, January 30, 1907, Box 694; B.C.E.R., *Annual Report*, 1907.
[26] A. P. Ingrame to Sperling, September 20, 1907, Box 673.
[27] Kidd to Sperling, November 30, 1910, Box 44–751; Sperling to H. Kirby, [September, 1912], LFGM; M. Urwin to F. Glover, October 5, 1912, Box 47B–845.
Horne-Payne's relationship with Mackenzie and Mann probably played no role in this. On the Saanich peninsula, the Canadian Northern and the B.C.E.R. competed as they did of course between New Westminster and Chilliwack. In another case, that of the Canadian Western Lumber Company, of which Horne-Payne as well as Mackenzie and Mann were directors, the B.C.E.R. would not extend its New Westminster city lines two miles to the mill site until the lumber company provided a free right of way and other concessions and until the B.C.E.R. was convinced that there was sufficient traffic to warrant the construction of the line.

decline in revenue on the Fraser Valley branch. Sperling and his officials were, like most British Columbians at the time, optimistic about the future. They blamed the fall in revenue on the unaggressive policy of the former traffic and transportation manager and on other temporary problems such as the failure of the fruit crop and a shortage of rolling stock. The board, however, correctly realized that the problem was the result of inflated real estate values which had discouraged settlement and farming. With the perspective of distance,[28] the board was able to see the whole picture unclouded by local enthusiasms.

In planning street railways on the mainland, the company had naturally concentrated on areas where there was likely to be immediate and profitable traffic, but the board had also sought to devise a building program which, if it did not forestall municipal competition, would at least mitigate its effects. Because of their British experience with municipal ownership of utilities, they were particularly sensitive to all talk of public ownership. They tried to obtain longterm franchises and to build some lines on private rights of way under a federal charter which would protect them from a municipal take-over.

Soon after Horne-Payne organized the B.C.E.R., the problem of negotiating franchises quickly showed the directors' domination of management and their concern for the security of the investment. The first of the short-term franchises which the B.C.E.R. had inherited from its predecessors was due for renewal in 1900. In principle, Horne-Payne agreed with Buntzen's proposal to increase the percentage of earnings paid to the city for the use of its streets in return for a consolidated franchise which would not expire until 1918. The board suggested, however, that the percentage should be based on net rather than gross earnings and that the franchise should be extended to 1929.[29] When the city refused to relinquish its right to purchase the lines, the negotiations stopped. Five months later, Buntzen recommended that the company might build one and one-half miles of street railway extensions requested by the city in return for a consolidated franchise. Although the city would accept this proposal, the board was unwilling to spend $15,000–$20,000 on extensions, and it believed that the city could be made to accept a lower percentage based on excess rather than gross earnings. In adopting the latter policy, the board was taking the advice

---

[28] Urwin to Sperling, March 9, 1912, Box 657; Sperling to Urwin, June 3, 1912, Box 51A–948–Fl; Alan Purvis to Sperling, May 25, 1912, Box 51A–948–Fl.

[29] Buntzen to Hope, August 3, 1899, Box 73; Board of Directors, Minutes, August 22, 1899 and September 12, 1899, Box 688.

of unnamed "friends" (probably Mackenzie and Mann) who had large electric railway interests elsewhere. Buntzen replied that under the excess earnings arrangement, the street railways of Toronto, Montreal, and Hamilton paid more to their respective cities than did the B.C.E.R. Already frustrated by the board's unwillingness to provide funds for extensions and improvements, Buntzen regarded the board's stand as a question of confidence and threatened to resign. The board cabled reassurances, authorized him to complete negotiations on the original terms — if delay would be dangerous — but urged him to stall discussions until Horne-Payne could visit Vancouver and personally examine the situation. Thus, Horne-Payne himself was responsible for the final agreement, which was similar to the original one proposed by Buntzen, who had been vindicated.[30]

The franchise question, especially as it related to the suburban municipalities, continued after R. H. Sperling became manager. The company sought to reduce the likelihood of the city of Vancouver's exercising its option to buy the street railway lines by surrounding the city with long-term suburban franchises. Without access to the suburbs, the city lines would lose much of their attractiveness. Once it had these long-term franchises, the B.C.E.R. was prepared to reduce their lifespan in return for an extension of the city franchise. Because long-term franchises were essential to the security of the investment, the board again carefully supervised these negotiations.

Recalling the relative ease with which they had secured forty and fifty-year franchises in South and North Vancouver respectively, the directors expected to obtain equally favorable terms from the other municipalities. They forgot that in those two municipalities they had been dealing mainly with real estate speculators who were anxious to get the street railway and electric lighting on almost any terms. In Point Grey, however, many of the ratepayers were firm believers in municipal ownership and were unwilling to grant a long-term franchise. If the B.C.E.R. would not accept their terms, they threatened to welcome competitors or build a municipally-owned tram line. The board, aware that either proposal would require the raising of funds in London, discounted the ability of a competitor, private or public, to challenge the B.C.E.R. Indeed, the board exercised a firm hand. Believing that the municipality

<hr/>

[30] Buntzen to T. F. McGuigan, February 11, 1901, CMLB; Buntzen to Hope, February 27, 1901, GMLB; Horne-Payne to Buntzen, April 3, 1901, Box 73; Buntzen to Horne-Payne, April 23, 1901, GMLB; Buntzen to Hope, May 18, 1901, Box 647; McGuigan to Buntzen, October 15, 1901, Box 637.

should come to the company rather than the other way round, it even refused to quote rates on electric power, though Sperling warned that this would give rise to a well-founded charge that the B.C.E.R. was a monopoly.[31]

In an attempt to develop good will in Point Grey and to promote settlement, Sperling voluntarily announced that he would reduce fares on the Vancouver and Lulu Island Railway [32] — an interurban line which ran through part of Point Grey — to make them equal to those charged on the main Vancouver-New Westminster interurban. Sperling had informed the board of his plan to reduce fares, but he made his public announcement before receiving their approval. The directors were annoyed. While denying the necessity of consultation on the fare question, they chided Sperling for not having waited for their decision after having asked for advice. Moreover, they disapproved of the policy. In a long letter they warned of the danger of setting equal rates for equal distances when circumstances varied. They argued that fares could be adjusted to promote development in particular areas, to bargain for bonuses, and "with a little dexterity to prove the evil results of short franchises which compelled companies to get higher rates during the short life of the franchise." The board accepted Sperling's decision to lower fares as a *fait accompli* but insisted that future policies on fares should be decided upon "by the Board with the assistance of management." [33]

The proposed franchise agreement, particularly its fifteen-year term, was equally displeasing. Since the B.C.E.R.'s only reason for building in Point Grey at that time was to get a franchise to use later in bargaining for a more favorable city franchise, Horne-Payne would not accept less than a forty-year term. He expected that if the company ignored Point Grey while building elsewhere, Point Grey residents would "very soon come to their senses and agree to our terms." The district was sparsely settled; Horne-Payne could wait. Within the year, a new municipal council offered a basic forty-year franchise in return for such concessions as a gradual reduction of fares. The board still feared that fare reductions would set a precedent and promote settlement in outer suburbs rather than in the more profitable inner ones, but they accepted Sperling's

<hr />

[31] Kidd to Sperling, October 17, 1908, Box 698; Sperling to Kidd, October 30, 1908, Box 23-331. For the B.C.E.R.'s dealings with the municipalities see Roy, "The Fine Arts," 250–51.

[32] This line was owned by the Canadian Pacific Railway but had been operated by the B.C.E.R. under a lease agreement since 1905.

[33] Kidd to Sperling, January 21, 1909, Box 26–368.

recommendations. After all, the agreement included their main concern — a long-term franchise.[34]

In another attempt to prevent the city from exercising its option to buy the street railway in 1919, the B.C.E.R. sought to consolidate its greater Vancouver franchises. During the tedious and complicated negotiations on the matter, the board again dominated policy making. In addition to the usual exchanges of letters and cables, several board members visited Vancouver. The most contentious matter was, again, the life of the franchise. The board wanted to make it at least thirty years; management officials, conscious of local political realities, were inclined to accept a shorter period. The board sent Buntzen, the managing director, to investigate. When he concurred with Sperling that it might be necessary to concede a twenty-three-year agreement, the board accepted the shorter term. Subsequently, Sperling, on his own initiative, offered additional concessions such as uniform light and power rates throughout the areas covered by the agreement. The board, however, refused to make any concessions beyond those approved at the time of Buntzen's visit without a full list of municipal requests and an estimate of their cost. It would not deal with the municipalities on a piecemeal basis.[35]

In the meantime, after a civic election, a new Vancouver city council asked Sperling for more concessions. The board considered these demands unreasonable and instructed him to withdraw from the discussions. A few months later, G. P. Norton, a director, visited the city but failed to revive the negotiations. When the city's franchise consolidation committee recommended that the city take over the street railway in 1919, the board told Sperling to plan measures which would make it "exceedingly difficult, if not impracticable for the City in 1919 to operate the City lines if they should acquire them." The Board had already advised him to reduce capital expenditures within the city as much as possible and to place the odium of refusing new work and improvements on them.[36]

Early in 1912 the B.C.E.R. revived the consolidation question with the Greater Vancouver Transportation Committee. Unlike the

[34] Kidd to Sperling, February 4, 1909, Box 699; Kidd to Sperling, April 1, 1909, Box 23–331; Sperling to Kidd, December 21, 1909, LFGM; Sperling to Kidd, January 20, 1910, London Letter Book, #7.

[35] B.C.E.R. (Vancouver) to B.C.E.R. (London), November 4, 1910, LFGM; B.C.E.R. (London) to B.C.E.R. Vancouver), November 7, 1910, LFGM; H. Williams to Sperling, February 25, 1911, Box 192.

[36] Williams to Glover, April 13, 1911, Box 192; Williams to Sperling, September 16, 1911, Box 192; Sperling to Williams, October 3, 1911, LFGM; Urwin to Sperling, November 22, 1911, Box 713.

former Franchise Consolidation Committee, this new body included representatives of the suburban municipalities as well as the city. When these negotiations terminated in "calm disorder" over the questions of fares, extension policies, and the percentage to be paid to the city,[37] the Vancouver *Province* in a generally friendly editorial declared: [38]

> It may be said frankly that some of the difficulties in dealing with this question arise from the fact that the B.C.E. Ry., like the Grand Trunk, has hitherto been directed by a London board. The disadvantages arising from this fact are obvious. The numerous questions and difficulties that inevitably arise with dealing with transportation in Greater Vancouver would probably be much better dealt with by resident than by non-resident directors, particularly if the boards were reinforced by men of business who have long lived here, who have seen the city and its outskirts grow, and who are therefore better able to judge of the necessities of the case than those who have merely a visiting knowledge, and some of them not even that.

The *Province* probably reflected public opinion, but the company was using its absentee board to good advantage to secure sound financing and to prevent over-expansion.

When the board learned that the Transportation Committee wanted "impossible" terms, it instructed management to start afresh, to ignore any previous concessions and to get the municipalities to "formulate their requirements as a whole for submission to [the] Board." Sperling was not to commit the company "to any concessions until approved by the Board." The directors claimed they were not dictating management's policy. Indeed, they wanted Sperling to have a "very free hand" and merely desired to give him an excuse to avoid dealing with the municipalities on a piecemeal basis — a system which the board regarded as a game of "squeeze." [39] In spite of its disclaimers, the board had really not relinquished any control over management. Whenever Sperling proposed any concessions, the board rejected them. Horne-Payne wanted a thirty-year franchise and a 5¼ per cent guarantee. He was, however, not completely inflexible. After a Vancouver alderman declared that a consolidation agreement could be reached on the basis of a twenty-three-year term, the board, in consultation with Sperling (who was visiting London), permitted the acting manager, G. R. G. Conway, to suggest a twenty-seven-year agreement provided other conditions

[37] Vancouver *Daily Province*, May 9, 1912, 24.
[38] June 18, 1912, 6.
[39] B.C.E.R. (London) to B.C.E.R. (Vancouver), February 21, 1912, Box 192; B.C.E.R. (London) to B.C.E.R. (Vancouver), February 22, 1912, Box 713; Urwin to general manager, March 1, 1912, Box 713.

were favorable. They did not, however, respond to Conway's requests for an outline of the best terms they would concede and for permission to make decisions on the matter without constant reference to London. In fact, the board reminded Conway of the desirability of keeping them informed by frequent cables.[40]

Moreover, Horne-Payne reiterated his intention to deal firmly with the municipalities and the provincial government. If the Transportation Committee did not immediately accept the twenty-seven-year franchise, the board advised Conway to announce a fare increase through the cancellation of cheap tickets and to blame the increase on rising costs, particularly those caused by the provincial government's new tramway regulations. Conway and his officials were horrified by the prospect of "open war" with the provincial government and the destruction of any possibility of reaching a consolidated franchise agreement. Although the board agreed to postpone the abolition of tickets and to accept a twenty-five-year franchise if other terms were satisfactory, it was not really worried about antagonizing the government. From its London vantage point it well knew that Premier McBride realized the financial implications of any retaliatory action his government might take.[41]

The board also knew that the prospect of Vancouver being able to raise the funds necessary to buy the street railway in 1919 was declining. The city had recently failed to float one of its bond issues on the London market.[42] When the municipalities could not agree among themselves and allowed the franchise consolidation scheme to fade into oblivion, the B.C.E.R. was not upset. Long-term suburban franchises and a superior financial position had secured its investment without the added insurance of a consolidated franchise. By using his intimate knowledge of the London money markets, the insulation of distance from local political pressures, and patience, Horne-Payne achieved his object of security for the investment without having made any of the concessions proposed by his managers.

Horne-Payne used similar methods when a private company seemed to threaten the B.C.E.R.'s monopoly of the light and power business on the Lower Mainland. In 1901, some Vancouver businessmen organized the Stave Lake Power Company to develop

[40] B.C.E.R. (Vancouver) to B.C.E.R. (London), July 1, 1912; B.C.E.R. (London) to B.C.E.R. (Vancouver), July 9, 1912; B.C.E.R. (Vancouver) to B.C.E.R. London), July 27, 1912; B.C.E.R. (Vancouver) to B.C.E.R. (London), August 30, 1912; B.C.E.R. (London) to G. R. G. Conway, September 10, 1912, Box 713.
[41] B.C.E.R. (Vancouver) to B.C.E.R. (London), September 11, 1912; B.C.E.R. (London) to Conway, September 16, 1912, Box 713.
[42] B.C.E.R. (London) to B.C.E.R. (Vancouver), March 8, 1912, Box 192.

cheap water power for sale to industrial users. There was considerable public sympathy for the new firm which might force the B.C.E.R. to reduce rates. During the next few years both Buntzen and Sperling feared that the Stave Lake Company might actually develop a hydro-electric power plant. Believing that the rival could not overcome its many financial problems, the board rejected any idea to buy it out unless it was actually in operation and refused to permit management to make any concessions to municipalities or customers as a means of forestalling competition. Then, Montreal interests reorganized the Stave Lake Company as the Western Canada Power Company and brought its plant into production. The board of the B.C.E.R. was concerned, but they knew that their superior financial position would enable them to defeat a rival in any price war.

Nevertheless, the board did not completely oppose negotiations with the Western Canada Power Company. In the winter of 1912 a shortage of rainfall and delays in completing one of the B.C.E.R.'s storage dams threatened its power supply. The board permitted Sperling to discuss the purchase of power from the Western Canada Company and participated itself in negotiations in London. In February 1913, the companies reached an agreement whereby the B.C.E.R. surrendered the industrial power business (which it had not developed), gained an additional power source without any capital expenditure through the purchase of bulk power from the W.C.P., and freed itself from competition in the profitable lighting and small power business. Moreover, the B.C.E.R. had not had to make any concessions to customers or to the municipalities which had attempted to play off the companies against each other. The board's financial knowledge and patience had again rewarded the B.C.E.R.

CONCLUSION

Horne-Payne's concern for the company's financial situation and his intimate knowledge of the money markets was a keystone of the B.C.E.R.'s success during its formative years. By carefully studying the state of the capital markets before deciding on any program of expansion, Horne-Payne provided the company with relatively cheap capital and enabled it, unlike many Canadian transportation enterprises, to be financially independent of government. To pursue this policy of giving primary attention to the company's finances, Horne-Payne and his directors had to exercise firm control over management officials. The manager was expected to carry on negotiations with local authorities and to make suggestions to the board, but he never had authority to make policy or to alter it without the approval of the directors. While the manager sometimes seemed to be little more than an errand boy, he was not simply a puppet. His recommendations were often adopted, even when they affected subjects which were clearly the responsibility of the board, such as the setting of dividends. The directors realized the need to maintain harmonious relations with the public the company served and recognized that their manager was more knowledgeable in this matter than they. Nevertheless, the needs of the company were always paramount over the wants of the customers.

Distance was an effective insulation against local pressures for new facilities and improved terms. In dealing with the municipalities of greater Vancouver, the board, with its awareness of the municipal and provincial financial situation, resisted many of management's suggestions for concessions to the municipalities. The same kind of information also permitted the board to forestall precipitate action following the appearance of a privately-owned competitor. Moreover, because the board was not bogged down by the minutiae of negotiations it could see a broad picture. It could suggest trading off concessions in one part of the business for the benefit of another and it could clearly see the long-term implications of policies. The directors were also able to offer advice based on much wider experience than any manager could hope to accumulate for himself. Part of their reluctance to build new lines was based on their knowledge that the multiplication of lines had had detrimental effects elsewhere. Occasionally, the board's experience led it to make unwise decisions. Their preoccupation with municipal franchise agreements was influenced by British examples of municipal ownership and the formation of the Hydro-Electric Power Commission of Ontario in 1906. This fear of municipal ownership contributed to the Saanich fiasco. Yet, strong franchises helped the company to raise its capital.

Probably the greatest advantage of the 6,000 miles between the board and their managers was the company's relative freedom from over-expansion caused by enthusiasm about future growth. This is clear when Horne-Payne's cautious policies for the B.C.E.R. are contrasted with the activities of Mackenzie and Mann, who had full control of their assorted endeavors. Canadian Northern policy, being made in Canada, was profoundly affected by the spirit of optimism summarized by Sir Wilfrid Laurier's declaration that "the twentieth century belongs to Canada." By 1905, with the help of government financial aid as well as funds raised through Horne-Payne, Mackenzie and Mann had abandoned any pretence of having a conservative attitude toward the building of new lines and began to turn their successful prairie railway into Canada's third transcontinental.[43] During World War I, while the B.C.E.R. experienced considerable trouble, it was never in any danger of insolvency. On the other hand, the federal government had to nationalize the Canadian Northern to prevent serious damage to Canada's credit by allowing it to go into receivership.

Indeed, in a rapidly developing and young economy, control of a company's activities by outsiders who are chiefly concerned with long-term investment prospects may be of greater benefit to all concerned than critics of absentee ownership would like to admit. By practicing direct management through an English board of directors, the B.C.E.R. saved a young community from its own inflated expectations. The B.C.E.R. was able to consider its financial security first and the wants of British Columbia second and, in the long run, to satisfy both. The directors of the B.C.E.R. turned the handicap of distance between London and British Columbia into the advantage of perspective which permitted their customers to enjoy the orderly growth of some basic public utilities while they ran the company "successfully and with profit."

[43] See T. D. Regehr, "The Canadian Northern Railway: The West's Own Product," *Canadian Historical Review*, LI (June, 1970), 177–187.

By *Alan Wilson*

PROFESSOR OF HISTORY

TRENT UNIVERSITY

Maritime Business History: A Reconnaissance of Records, Sources, and Prospects

❡ *Professor Wilson surveys existing materials for the historical study of business in Canada's Maritime provinces and considers the outlook for future studies of that region.*

Canada's Maritime Provinces — Nova Scotia, New Brunswick, and Prince Edward Island — are set apart from the rest of the country, and have undergone a separate historical experience.[1] Only Quebec can claim the depth of tradition and early roots evidenced in the Maritimes. Only Quebec rivals their rural image and reflects a similar level of poverty, limited industrial progress, and detachment from the common continental pattern of material advance and bustle.

The Maritimes are the least continental part of Canada, and in the leading early interpretive synthesis of Canada's history, they played almost no role. This Laurentian thesis was based on two elements: the economic implications of the exploitation of the staples of fur, timber, and wheat; and the progressively westward course of this developmental pattern from the St. Lawrence river ports of Quebec and Montreal, via the Ottawa River and Great Lakes system, and thence by the great east-west river systems of the West. In this enterprise the metropolitan thrust of Montreal, so brilliantly developed by Donald Creighton in his *Commercial Empire of the St. Lawrence*, was unparalleled. The entrepreneurial expansion of Toronto and Winnipeg followed somewhat later and was related to industrial as well as commercial ambitions. The Maritimes, however, were shut out from a similar economic metropolitanism in the vast continental hinterland, and from the ties with British imperial financial history as evidenced by Montreal's business community.

Moreover, to the scholar who inspired the Laurentian thesis,

Business History Review, Vol. XLVII, No. 2 (Summer, 1973). Copyright © The President and Fellows of Harvard College.

[1] I have not included Newfoundland or the fairly recent idea of the "Atlantic Provinces" (which includes Newfoundland), for Newfoundland's history is peculiar unto itself — especially in economic and business history.

Harold Adams Innis, the dispersal of Maritime enterprise in scattered fishing ports and isolated lumbering camps and towns meant that metropolitan centers grew up with difficulty.[2] Individual initiative and local enterprise were the strong characteristics of such a socio-economic pattern. The strategic naval placement of the Crown settlement of Halifax, and St. John's location at the mouth of its mighty river, gave those cities much of their distinction. Their pre-eminence did not, then, reflect a commercial or industrial hegemony typical of continental metropolitan models. Not until the twentieth century did Halifax assert and establish its position as a metropolitan financial center within the Maritime or Canadian scene.

In the eighteenth and nineteenth centuries many smaller towns such as Moncton, St. Stephen, Yarmouth, and Pictou had their own metropolitan ambitions, extending not only to neighboring villages and rural hinterlands but even to the prospect of establishing positions in the trans-Atlantic carrying trade. These dreams persisted even beyond Confederation, when more advantaged central Canadian industrial and commercial competitors might have been expected to win an early victory. Moreover, because no single staple dominated many of these Maritime centers — or because their basic staple was the sea and its manifold possibilities — their commercial and industrial activities were surprisingly varied and complex. Single entrepreneurs, families of astonishing economic versatility, and combinations of merchant-shipper interests (such as Yarmouth's "Long Wharf" clique) continued at least until the early years of the twentieth century to pursue complex careers of finance, commerce, industry, and politics. By the late twentieth century, their numbers have become sharply reduced, but the genus is still easily recognizable in the Maritimes in such figures as the Irvings, Jodreys, Sobeys, and MacCullochs.[3]

OPPORTUNITIES FOR STUDY

Indeed, few areas of comparable population offer such a varied potential to the business historian. The region provides samples of

[2] "An Introduction to the Economic History of the Maritimes, including Newfoundland and New England," in Harold A. Innis, *Essays in Canadian Economic History*, ed. by Mary Q. Innis (Toronto, 1956), 27–42.

[3] K. C. Irving and his sons dominate New Brunswick's petroleum refining and marketing, shipbuilding, transport, and newspaper industries; Roy Jodrey, President of Minas Basin Pulp & Paper Co. Ltd., Chairman of the Board of Canadian Keyes Fibre Co. Ltd., and Vice-President of the Canadian Permanent Trust Co., is director and a large-scale investor in numerous regional and national enterprises; Frank Sobey, Chairman of the Board of Sobeys Stores Ltd., a major regional grocery chain, is prominent on many company boards and past Chairman of Nova Scotia's entrepreneurial crown corporation, Industrial Estates Ltd.; Charles MacCulloch, President of Nova Scotia's leading lumber and hardware chain,

vast monopolies and personal fiefdoms in which economic interests merge with great social and political power. There is also a bewildering variety of business activity owned and conducted by "foreign" interests following take-over patterns by American fishing interests since the 1920s; by central Canadian iron and steel absorptions of Nova Scotia enterprises; by later "Canadian" incursions of department and grocery store chains such as Eaton's;[4] by Scandinavian and Japanese automobile projects with heavy governmental subventions, and buttressed by provincial "nationalization" of electrical production in a region commonly lacking a single elected socialist representative. Cooperative fisheries enterprises, such as in the Baptist community of Port Bickerton, Nova Scotia, suggest the relevance of religious values to economic enterprise on both a communal and individual level. There is also abundant evidence of the continuation of traditional small industrial or commercial undertakings. These remain stubbornly independent and are maintained partly at an optimal social level (rather than at a maximal level of business productivity) with a high degree of morale among a comparatively low-paid staff, whose executives count it a necessary fringe benefit to reserve Wednesday afternoons for golf.

Indeed, the subject of entrepreneurship should have a special attraction for Maritime historians and biographers. The Maritimes have long offered opportunities to some native sons to build power and wealth at home, yet as Professor Roy George has suggested,[5] the immigration of entrepreneurial skills from central Canada to the Maritimes and recent limitations upon effective entrepreneurship in a branch-plant economy have posed serious problems for the native businessman. Moreover, for every successful native entrepreneur remaining in the region, dozens have migrated to other parts of Canada, to the United States, or to Britain. An important field of study awaits in the area of capital and entrepreneurial immigration and emigration, and of the peculiar atmosphere of the Maritimes that appears to breed the measure of ambition, singleness of purpose, and adaptability so successfully displayed by such expatriate Maritimers as Lord Beaverbrook, Isaac Killam, Cyrus Eaton, Sir James Dunn of Algoma Steel, Henry Borden of Brazilian Traction, Peter McColough of Xerox, even of W. A. C. Bennett, who dis-

---

MacCullochs Ltd., is also an outstanding figure in Halifax real estate and construction enterprises, and currently is Chairman of Industrial Estates Ltd.

[4] In the 1930s my father, a Halifax wholesale grocer, considered that the Maritimes faced three equally-matched evils — Hitler, the C.C.F., and Dominion Stores.

[5] Roy E. George, *A Leader or a Laggard: Manufacturing Industry in Nova Scotia, Quebec and Ontario* (Toronto, 1970).

played similar entrepreneurial skills as a merchant and as the long-time premier of British Columbia.

The Maritimes should, then, be a mine to the business historian interested in exploring the broader dimensions of business history related to social and cultural values, political connections, multinational patterns, regional characteristics, and the problems and sources of entrepreneurship. Maritime business operations have so often been local and family oriented that secondary and other corroborative materials in family histories, memoirs, and diaries may be especially helpful in the reconstruction of business history. The marked regional inter-connections of business, society, and politics should project business history in the Maritimes into a wider dimension *sui generis*.

A more direct factor should also prompt Maritime business studies. Dissatisfaction with the economic and fiscal terms of Confederation has been a continuing theme in the Maritimes since the 1860s. Although a movement to unite the Maritimes in that period was not widely supported, Maritime business leaders were among the most outspoken opponents of Confederation with the Canadas. Subsequently, the origins of the "Better Terms" movement — the demand for improved tariff and fiscal arrangements within the Confederation — and for "Maritime Rights" rested with businessmen, and have attracted business support for over a century. The subject has deep regional and local significance, and sporadic attempts to improve regional bargaining power with Ottawa through Maritime Union have regularly prompted mixed responses from the business community. This complex subject deserves the attention of business historians, for it remains alive to this moment.

A resurgence of interest in Maritime Union in the late 1960s is not likely to result in political union, but efficiency and economy may be achieved by increasing inter-provincial coordination of government services. Regular Maritime Premiers' Conferences continue to explore such administrative changes, which must substantially affect the patterns and interests of business, for example, in the reduction of conflicting provincial industrial development commissions and crown corporations; by common agricultural production and marketing regulations; through technical education and common labour codes; by coordination of fisheries subsidization and anti-pollution control; in common bargaining with Ottawa in fiscal matters and over such sensitive issues as off-shore oil and mineral rights; and in bureaucratic or capital site rearrangements consequent on any advance toward administrative or political union. These questions must affect and reflect regional, metropolitan, urban, business, and economic interests. Their exploration in a historical and business context should contribute to their proper understanding and to the preparation of informed decisions. Micro-business history in the Maritimes in the form of simple "company histories" may not develop very swiftly, partly from the lack of records; but macro-history — business in a broader economic, entrepreneurial, social, political, and cultural context — offers splendid prospects.

PROBLEMS IN MARITIME STUDIES

At the moment, however, there are handicaps as well as opportunities. The business historian has at hand no readily available framework of political, social, or even economic history. There is no history of Prince Edward Island after 1831; no modern history of New Brunswick extends beyond Confederation in 1867; and there has been no comprehensive history of Nova Scotia attempted since 1873. This situation might be wholly discouraging were it not that a surprising number of older, specialized studies of Canadian and Maritime economic and business activity are still available in scattered libraries. These include many earlier Canadian and British articles and monographs,[6] and lately a developing body of New England studies in immigration, lumbering, fishing, shipping, and industry that impinges helpfully on the Maritimes by tracing New

[6] See, for example, F. W. Johnson, *Report on the Agricultural Capabilities of . . . New Brunswick* (Fredericton, 1850); S. J. MacLean, *The Tariff History of Canada* (Toronto, 1895); Chalfant Robinson, *Two Reciprocity Treaties* (New Haven, 1903); W. O. Raymond, *History of the St. John River* (Saint John, 1905); J. Hannay, *History of New Brunswick*, 2 vols. (Saint John, 1909); C. O. MacDonald, *The Coal and Iron Industries of Nova Scotia* (n.d.); B. E. Fernow, *Forest Conditions in Nova Scotia* (Ottawa, 1912); W. J. A. Donald, *The Canadian Iron and Steel Industry* (Boston, 1915); H. Michell, *The Cooperative Store in Canada* (Kingston, 1916); R. Drummond, *Minerals and Mining in Nova Scotia* (Stellarton, 1918); Basil Lubbock, *The Colonial Clippers* (London, 1921); F. L. Benns, *The American Struggle for the British West Indies Carrying Trade, 1815–30* (Bloomington, Ind., 1923); R. G. Albion, *Forests and Sea Power* (Cambridge, Mass., 1926); R. F. Grant, *The Canadian Atlantic Fishery* (Toronto, 1934); *The Maritime Provinces, 1867–1934* (Dominion Bureau of Statistics, 1934); D. C. Masters, *The Reciprocity Treaty of 1854* (Toronto, 1936); J. B. Brebner, *The Neutral Yankees of Nova Scotia* (N.Y., 1937); A. R. M. Lower, *The North American Assault on the Canadian Forest* (Toronto, 1938); Norman Macdonald, *Canada, 1763–1841, Immigration and Settlement* (London, 1939); G. S. Graham, *Sea Power and British North America, 1783–1820* (Cambridge, 1941) and his *Empire of the North Atlantic* (Toronto, 1946); H. A. Innis, ed., *The Diary of Simeon Perkins, 1776–1780* (Toronto, 1948), and succeeding volumes edited by D. C. Harvey and C. B. Fergusson; A. H. Clark, *Three Centuries and the Island* [P.E.I] (Toronto, 1959); G. R. Stevens, *Canadian National Railways*, I (Toronto, 1960); and L. Manny, *Ships of the Miramichi* (Saint John, 1960). Articles are too numerous for useful reduction here, but they appear in a wide range of journals including the *Dalhousie Review, New England Quarterly, Canadian Historical Review, Acadiensis* [new and old versions], and the *Collections* of various regional historical societies. I am preparing a check list of articles that will be available to interested students.

England's historic economic imperialism and interaction with the Maritimes.[7]

Another vein, although of uneven quality, runs through university libraries in the Maritimes and beyond in unpublished, frequently forgotten M.A. theses on specialized aspects of Maritime trade, shipping, or industrial activity.[8] Although many are immature productions, they often have the virtue of the patient exhumation of facts and data upon which the business historian may put his own construction. Provincial legislative and federal parliamentary debates and journals, together with innumerable reports and research papers of royal commissions, provincial and federal, are a further obvious source of published materials. Nor are the published governmental sources confined to Canada: British parliamentary papers of the nineteenth century, such as the "Report from the Select Committee on British Shipping, 1844," provide important perspectives on colonial shipping, shipbuilding, and trading activity.

Of other published sources there is a mixed bag, varying from early nineteenth-century immigrants' guides, which combine natural history, settlers' accounts, and progress reports, to twentieth-century promotional and commemorative accounts. For Nova Scotia, these range from John McGregor's 1828 *Historical and Descriptive Sketches of the Maritime Provinces* and John Homer's *Brief Sketch*

[7] See, for example, such important works as Harold Davis, *An International Community on the St. Croix* (Orono, Me., 1950); Joseph Malone, *Pine Trees and Politics: The Naval Stores and Forest Policy in Colonial New England* (Seattle, 1964); John Ahlin, *Maine Rubicon: Downeast Settlers During the American Revolution* (Calais, Me., 1966); George Rawlyk, *Yankees at Louisbourg* (Orono, Me., 1967); and David Smith, *Lumbering and the Maine Woods: A Bibliographical Guide* (Portland, Me., 1971).

[8] A few of the most useful M.A. theses are listed below. *Acadia University*: R. M. Guy, "Industrial Development and Urbanization of Pictou Co., N.S. to 1900" (1962); *Dalhousie University*: F. G. Butler, "Commercial Relations of Nova Scotia with the United States, 1783–1830" (1932); W. R. Copp, "Nova Scotia and the War of 1812" (1935); R. D. Evans, "Transportation and Communication in Nova Scotia, 1815–1850" (1936); A. A. Lomas, "The Industrial Development of Nova Scotia, 1830–1854" (1950); Colin Howell, "Repeal, Reciprocity and Commercial Union in Nova Scotian Politics" (1967); J. A. Maxwell, "A Financial History of Nova Scotia"; A. MacKenzie, "The Rise and Fall of the Farm Labour Party in Nova Scotia" (1969); A. MacKenzie, "The Rise and Fall of the Farm Labour Party in Nova Scotia" (1969); *Mount Allison University*: W. M. MacLeod, "The Economic Problems of the New Brunswick Acadia Coal Company" (1938); *University of New Brunswick*: A. W. Bailey, "Railways in New Brunswick, 1827–1867" (1955); R. C. Campbell, "Symonds, Hazen and White: A Study of a New Brunswick Firm in the Commercial World of the Eighteenth Century" (1970); J. K. Chapman, "Relations of Maine and New Brunswick in the Era of Reciprocity, 1849–1867" (1952); D. W. Gallagher, "The Commercial Fisheries of New Brunswick, 1926–1953" (1955); H. M. Grant, "Northumberland County; An Estimate of its Wealth and Income" (1941); E. H. Greaves, "Peter Mitchell, A Father of Confederation" (1958); W. H. Harrison, "The Maritime Bank of the Dominion of Canada, 1872–1887" (1970); G. Hazenberg, "An Analysis of the New Brunswick Lumber Industry" (1966); D. F. MacGowan, "Clifton, New Brunswick: The Rise and Fall of a Shipbuilding Community" (1955); R. MacLellan, "Income Fluctuations of Potato Producers in New Brunswick and Prince Edward Island, 1926–1958" (1960); F. B. MacMillan, "Trade of New Brunswick with Great Britain, the United States and the Caribbean, 1784–1849" (1955); R. W. Nablo, "Social Structure Related to Business and Finance in a Seaport City [St. John]" (1900); D. L. Poynter, "Economics and Politics of New Brunswick, 1878–1883" (1961); J. R. Rice, "A History of Organized Labour in Saint John, New Brunswick, 1813–1890" (1968); D. W. Smith, "The Maritime Years of R. B. Bennett, 1870–1897" (1968); Carl Wallace, "The Life and Times of Sir Albert James Smith" (1960).

of the *Present State of the Province of Nova Scotia*, a shipping agent's account of 1834, to modest business histories such as that of the Halifax shipping supply and hardware firm of William Stairs, Son and Morrow; [9] or the Halifax grocery and ship chandlery firm of Wentzells Ltd.; [10] a 1916 regional, industrial and historical survey of the steel towns of New Glasgow, Stellarton, Westville, and Trenton; [11] or a historical mining account published by the Nova Scotia Steel and Coal Company to commemorate the convention at Sydney in 1908 of the Canadian Mining Institute.[12] For New Brunswick, Peter Fisher's 1825 *Sketches of New-Brunswick* provided the immigrant with a rich collection of descriptive, historical, and statistical information from which the business historian can extrapolate a useful picture of trade and related fiscal and economic information; a useful early assessment is I. Cornwall's *The Cities of Saint John and Portland and the Woods and Wooden Manufactures of New Brunswick*, 1884; the growth of the Campobello fisheries is reflected in a memoir published in 1892 by Boston's Campobello Company; a year later, building on James Hannay's 1875 *St. John and Its Businesses*, John Hamilton's *St. John and the Province of New Brunswick* offered a wealth of information on businesses, commercial statistics, transport facilities, business directories, and biographical sketches of leading men in the business community; similar commemoratives were published in the early twentieth century for St. John, Moncton, and Sackville — all of great potential use to the business historian because they deal with significant towns across a wide span of time.[13]

Several other more authoritative published accounts exist, however, for Nova Scotia, including two classic early nineteenth-century compendia: T. C. Haliburton's 1829 *An Historical and Statistical Account of Nova Scotia in Two Volumes* and Abraham Gesner's 1849 *The Industrial Resources of Nova Scotia*, which went beyond descriptions of existing factories, commerce, and industry to elaborate the province's prospective economic developments, based on a dis-

[9] W. J. Stairs, *History of Stairs Morrow* (Halifax, 1906).

[10] *The Years Between; Halifax 1820–1923* (Halifax, 1923), which suggests the significance of the naval and military establishments for local suppliers.

[11] *New Glasgow's Industrial Centre, New Glasgow, Stellarton, Westville, Trenton; Birthplace of Steel in Canada* ([New Glasgow?] 1916).

[12] *Nova Scotia Steel and Coal Co. Ltd. Souvenir, 1908* ([New Glasgow?] 1908).

[13] *The Book of Saint John* (Saint John, 1903), a Board of Trade commemorative on the visit of Imperial Chambers of Commerce; *An Historical Sketch, 1783–1909* (Saint John, 1909), a tailoring company's commemorative; H. H. Steeves, *The Story of Moncton's First Store and Storekeeper* (Saint John, 1924); *Historic Moncton* (Moncton, 1934), histories of business firms, institutions, and of Moncton's strategic transport site; F. W. Wallace, *The Romance of a Great Port* (Saint John, 1935), a Silver Jubilee commemorative; and Charles Moffatt, *Introducing Sackville* (Sackville, 1946).

tinguished natural scientist's insights. On the eve of Confederation a particularly useful source is T. F. Knight, *Nova Scotia and Her Resources* (Halifax, 1862). In the 1870s, two further works of a parallel nature appeared: Duncan Campbell's 1873 *Nova Scotia, in Its Historical, Mercantile and Industrial Relations,* which concluded with six chapters devoted to the province's past and future in agriculture, mining, fisheries, immigration, and manufacturing; and G. A. White's 1876 *Halifax and Its Business,* an historical and contemporary account of the city's trade, including shipping, cordage manufacturing, publishing, and descriptions of its leading firms. Similar historical and current assessments appeared later for several of the province's other towns, notably in 1902 John Lawson's *Yarmouth Past and Present,* which embraced the county and much of southwestern Nova Scotia and was based on shipping records, business biographies and histories, and commercial statistics drawn from Lawson's *Yarmouth Herald* since 1831. Of similar authority and usefulness for the last half of the nineteenth century, however, were the three chief directories of the day: Luke Hutchinson's Halifax and Dartmouth *Directory* for 1863, and his Nova Scotia *Directory* for 1864–1865; the Toronto publication, *Our Dominion,* published in 1887 and 1889, which outlined the commercial and industrial activity of representative Maritime towns, together with accounts of leading firms and business leaders; and David McAlpine's *Maritime Provinces Directory* for 1870–1871, 1892, 1897, 1898, 1904, and 1911, which combined current information with historical sketches of business growth by province, county, and town. A few distinguished regional studies in the twentieth century [14] have also illustrated the usefulness of such sources as: Morgan's *Canadian Men and Women of the Time*; Parker's *Who's Who and Why*; Rose's *Cyclopedia of Canadian Biography*; the *Canadian Biographical Dictionary*; *Monetary Times*; *Canadian Journal of Commerce*; *Industrial Canada*; *The Canadian Magazine*; *Canadian Manufacturer*; the *Annual Financial Review*; the records of the debates and journals of the House of Commons; Commons' committee reports; the decennial census reports; and the principal Maritime, Toronto, and Montreal newspapers, where there regularly appeared references to Maritime businessmen and firms, or to central Canadian interest in expanding into the Maritimes. Invitations to consider such expansion have frequently appeared in informative and promotional

[14] Notably, T. W. Acheson's Toronto doctoral thesis (1972), "The Social Origins of Canadian Industrialism: A Study in the Structure of Entrepreneurship," and R. M. Guy's unpublished M.A. thesis, "Industrial Development and Urbanization of Pictou Co., N.S. to 1900" (Acadia University, 1962).

bulletins published, for example, by the Canadian National Railway since the 1930s. These present statistics and estimates of the industrial and commercial facilities and potential of sub-regions within the Maritime Provinces,[15] and must be of considerable value to the business and economic historian.

For New Brunswick specifically, while *Our Dominion* and the directories of Hutchinson and McAlpine are as valuable as for Nova Scotia, Gesner produced a companion study in 1847, *New Brunswick; With Notes for Immigrants*, and three years earlier W. C. Atkinson had brought out his *Historical and Statistical Account of New-Brunswick*. In the twentieth century, the *Maritime Merchant* and three successive and related journals — *The Busy East, The Maritime Advocate*, and *The Atlantic Advocate* — have regularly published feature articles and shorter accounts of community, company, or biographical material on economic history and prospects. Mainly concerned with New Brunswick, they are uneven in quality — ranging from rare scholarly productions through sound professional journalism to undisguised community promotion and pathetic regional hagiography, but they are not to be ignored. Although Hutchinson and McAlpine extended their labours to Prince Edward Island, there appear to be few other published sources to which the business historian of the Island can turn beyond Commons *Debates*, legislative accounts, committee reports, and newspaper materials.

Even in Nova Scotia, however, royal commission reports and supporting papers are not always readily available in public depositories, although access can usually be arranged through appropriate government departments. Exemplary research studies prepared for royal commissions constitute significant landmarks in Maritime economic and business history, such as Eugene Forsey's *Economic and Social Aspects of the Nova Scotia Coal Industry*, prepared for the 1926 Report of the Royal Commission on Maritime Claims; Alexander Brady's *Report on Electric Power*, prepared for the 1944 Report of the Royal Commission on Provincial Development and Rehabilitation; Donald Creighton's *British North America at Confederation*, prepared for the 1939 Report of the Royal Commission on Dominion-Provincial Relations [Rowell-Sirois]; and E. M. Saunders' *The Economic History of the Maritime Provinces*, prepared for the 1935 Report of the Royal Commission on Financial

---

[15] See, for example, "Canadian National Railways. An Industrial Survey of Lower Gloucester County [N.B.]" (1962); or "Canadian National Railways. An Industrial Survey of Fredericton . . . with Notes on Marysville and Oromocto" (1961).

Arrangements between the Dominion and the Maritime Provinces.

Another possible resource is the collection of the Atlantic Provinces Transportation Commission, located in Moncton. This Commission, authorized both by the provincial governments and the region's chambers of commerce, was established in the 1920s; it has since regularly collected studies, reports, and articles bearing directly on Maritime transportation interests. Although the Commission disclaims any pretence to offering a comprehensive reference library, on matters arising out of the Maritime Freight Rates Act its collection is the most complete in the country. But it is also a mine for students of "Maritime Rights" — a subject by no means limited in scope or period. Indeed, the Commission is itself a product of the pressure group represented by the chambers of commerce of the 1920s in demanding "Maritime Rights." In the frequent absence of systematic collections of local chamber or board of trade records in particular localities — another valuable tool — this depository is invaluable to the general economic, business, and political historian of the Maritimes. Although the history and resources of the more recently established Atlantic Provinces Economic Council have in some respects been more limited than those of the Transportation Commission, they too are willing to accommodate the business historian, and to put him in touch with experts in his field and with members of APEC's research committees, whose own knowledge and records may be of assistance to him. Among their own publications, A. C. Parks' "The Atlantic Provinces in Relation to the Canadian Economy, 1867–1955" (A.P.E.C., 1955) is a good example of their usefulness for the business historian. Indeed, it could be hoped that APEC might be prepared to play a coordinating role in the development of economic and business studies, for its own reputation for cooperation with the business community might be useful in alerting individuals and corporations to the dangers of continuing to permit their records to go uncatalogued and unpreserved.

A wide field of general economic and business history lies open to development in the Maritimes. A rash of recent theses on subjects relating to Maritime economic and business history may suggest that younger scholars are turning to the field. Many of these are M.A. dissertations, however, and the attrition rate to further studies is high, while frequently doctoral candidates do not persist in subjects related to their M.A. interests on leaving the Maritimes for larger graduate schools. Some encouragement may be taken, however, from the fact that several central Canadian scholars have recently turned their attention to Maritime metropolitan and business studies.[16] It is to be hoped that this initiative and the recent establishment by the University of New Brunswick's History Department of a scholarly journal of the history of the Atlantic region, *Acadiensis,* will mark another advance.[17] *Acadiensis* has already given proof of its interest in economic and business history, and its dedication to regional studies ought to serve as a spur to interested business historians.

ARCHIVAL SOURCES

Before publication, however, every historian faces the problem of consulting original materials and of depending upon major archival collections. For Maritime business studies this presents an awesome hurdle. In Prince Edward Island an Archives Act and an archivist are very recent additions to the provincial establishment. Preliminary collections and cataloguing of public records have been barely begun. Moreover, many papers — particularly of the nineteenth century — will simply not be found. Municipal records have not been catalogued or consolidated by the provincial archives, but some promise appears that they may be reasonably intact. A recent enquiry in the provincial holdings, however, revealed no corporate records and very few family or personal accounts of direct interest to the business historian. The collections and archives of the University of Prince Edward Island do not extend to business records or to personal or family papers in the field. Preparations for P.E.I.'s Confederation Centennial in 1973 and the consequent creation of a provincial Heritage Foundation have prompted further systematic searches, but officials are not optimistic about the discovery of significant business papers. The Island's preoccupation with agriculture and fishing in this century, and the presence of large administrative and experimental establishments — federal and provincial — may

[16] Professor J. M. S. Careless, of the University of Toronto, one of the country's most outstanding scholars and the inspirer of a new metropolitan school of Canadian history, is the most prominent figure in this connection. Careless's student, T. W. Acheson of the University of New Brunswick, has completed an important doctoral dissertation with valuable material on the post-Confederation Maritimes, "The Social Origins of Canadian Industrialism: A Study in the Structure of Entrepreneurship" (Toronto 1972), and a significant article, "The National Policy and the Industrialization of the Maritimes, 1880–1910," *Acadiensis,* I (Spring, 1972), 3–28. Another of Careless's students, now at Dalhousie University, D. A. Sutherland, is completing a promising doctoral study of "The Mercantile Community in Halifax in the 19th Century." Valuable examinations of business, commercial pressure groups and labour movements in the Maritimes are also under way in Ontario at Queen's and Trent Universities.

[17] See the provocative article by George Rawlyk, "A New Golden Age of Maritime Historiography?", *Queen's Quarterly,* 76 (1969), 55–65.

mean, however, that government records will prove to be especially useful in the absence of family and business collections. Fortunately, the archival situation is less depressing in the other Maritime provinces.

University libraries in New Brunswick are not, by policy or circumstance, at present major depositories of business records. The University of New Brunswick at the provincial capital of Fredericton does, however, hold a few important collections of interest to business historians.[18] Municipal and county records are being progressively consolidated in the Provincial Archives in Fredericton, although transfers are far from complete. The New Brunswick Historical Society has produced some brief articles of value to business historians,[19] but few concerning the post-Confederation period. Its early collections of manuscript materials are housed in the Archives Division of the New Brunswick Provincial Museum in Saint John, and they include a number of important business collections. The province's few local historical societies have been relatively more successful in this regard. The York Sunbury Society's papers and records are lodged with the Provincial Archives, and these include useful local records of prominent commercial families and a few business records, happily some from the twentieth century. Although the Charlotte County Historical Society has no original collection, it has produced several papers on local industrial development (such as Ganong's candy works, Short's shipyards, and a useful study of local grist mills); these are usually in typescript and are housed in the Provincial Museum's Archives Division.

No schools or department of business history or administration exist in New Brunswick's universities, and only a few scholars in university history departments have pursued an interest in business history.[20] There are, however, two principal archival centers in New Brunswick of interest to the business historian. The Archives Division of the New Brunswick Museum in St. John contains a vast miscellany of public and private historical records, including many items of value to students of provincial and local Saint

[18] The best papers include: Loggie, A. & R. Company (1886–1966), wholesale fish dealers, business correspondence (Chatham); Gilmour & Rankin (1851–93), papers of leading shipbuilders and lumber merchants (Douglastown); Mitchell, Peter (1854–1862), correspondence of a major shipbuilder and political figure (Newcastle).
[19] Notably J. R. H. Wilbur, "The Stormy History of the Maritime Bank," N.B.H.S. *Collections*, No. 19, 69 (1966).
[20] Notably Professors Wilbur and Acheson, and Professor William Spray — all of whom have been associated with U.N.B. In P.E.I. and Nova Scotia, business history can count no academic historians in its ranks at present. Academic economists in each province, however, have participated in examining the general economic and specific agricultural, industrial, and commercial development in the Maritime region, particularly for the twentieth century.

John economic activity. No attempt has been made to encourage the systematic collection of business materials, however, and the Division's 1967 "Inventory of Manuscripts" neither distinguishes nor evaluates such records.

The Museum's holdings, unfortunately, contain few business records sufficiently complete to warrant "company histories" of any note or comprehensiveness. For Saint John there are considerable papers, however, of the lumbering firm of Gregory's; of another Gregory firm of stevedores; of the hardware merchant family of Jarvis and their operations over several generations; of the Parker family of nearby Tynemouth Creek, sawyers, shipbuilders, and marine outfitters in the mid-nineteenth century; of the Sackville general merchandise and importing firm of Crane & Allison; of the Saint John merchant and farming family of Merritt; of the early shipbuilding, repair, and lumbering firm of Hilyard Bros.; of the early ship's masters family of Leavitt; of the Perth general merchant, lumberman, and politician of the mid-nineteenth century, G. T. Baird; of the prominent Saint John family of Hazens, whose interests were tied to land matters and to the significant Simonds, Hazen & White Company, combining shipping and trading interests with New England; and perhaps most notably, the Parks family papers, late nineteenth-century leaders in groceries, dry goods, and the important Saint John and New Brunswick Cotton Mills companies.

In addition, the Museum holds important records of the Saint John Board of Trade, including minute books; detailed accounts of city and county industrial exhibitions; scattered labor union records; the minutes of the Saint John City Council; scattered shipping records and logbooks; and useful scrapbooks on Saint John commerce, industry, and business leaders. The usefulness of the collection to business historians is clearly less than could be desired; in the absence to date of a policy of business collections, however, it may be surprising to researchers how much material has been preserved. Supplemented by the new Provincial Archives, the Museum's holdings will prove of great value to students of New Brunswick's economic record.[21]

[21] I have examined all of these materials, and aside from these general observations would be happy to provide more detailed descriptions and valuations to interested students.

The Museum's Archives Division served de facto as New Brunswick's archives until 1968, when the former library building of the University of New Brunswick was designated the Provincial Archives. Michael Swift, the Provincial Archivist, faces a mountainous task, for in addition to the delicate problem of overlapping jurisdictions and collections in the old Saint John Museum and the new Fredericton Archives, the Public Documents Dispersal Act of 1963 in effect created a government records management and disposal policy. In so doing it forced the early archivists to accept the primacy of governmental collections

The new Provincial Archives has itself already begun the accumulation of several important collections of business records. In addition, the Archives has published a guide to published works on New Brunswick's history: Hugh Taylor, *New Brunswick History, A Checklist of Secondary Sources* (Fredericton, 1971). Taylor's checklist is an indispensable reference work for business historians; regular supplements should be published reflecting new additions to archival holdings and published works.

The Archives collection includes governmental records touching on such matters as public works, contracts, agriculture, and financial and banking reports at the provincial level. There are also some good runs of county records, and particularly of extensive municipal records of Fredericton, Moncton, St. Stephen, and Newcastle — indicating real estate values, insurance company records, transport arrangements, local commercial and industrial exhibitions, etc. A special collection of Supreme Court bankruptcy materials provides a valuable and comprehensive record of such enterprises as the early twentieth-century Nepisiquit Lumber Company (Bathurst); the Saint John Building Society (1861–1888); the Maritime Bank (1873–1875); and the Cushing Sulphite Fiber Company (1899–1905). A few company collections are of interest, particularly the large Todd collection of the noted St. Stephen family of timber dealers, shippers, bankers, and cotton manufacturers. In addition, some family papers yield important business and banking materials, especially the vast and newly acquired Burchill papers, the record of an important South Nelson lumbering enterprise; the Gillmor papers, illustrating the complex business and political career of the Provincial Secretary of the Confederation period; the Elkins papers, scattered records on Miramichi immigration, lumbering, and shipping activities; the Samuel papers, the records of the mid-nineteenth-century merchant, shipper, and credit agent of the North Shore; and the Wood papers, concerned with the business, railroad, and political interests of the prominent Sackville businessman, Josiah Wood.

---

over private and corporate materials. Business and related private records, however, are constantly disappearing.

Perhaps some temporary alleviation can be provided by interested university faculty members, library staff, and local historical societies in supplementing the Archives' efforts to recover business materials. It may also be sensible for the Museum in Saint John to concentrate its business records retrieval programme upon metropolitan Saint John, transferring present holdings and future responsibilities for other sections of the province to the new Archives in Fredericton. Certainly, the prospect of a common provincial depository for government and corporate records would seem the most attractive. Moreover, recognition of Saint John's special place in the province's business and public life would be well served by a programme of concentrating Saint John's metropolitan records under the Museum's enterprising direction, but with the Archives' advice and cooperation.

It is to be hoped that the Archives may be able to secure further records of such prominent figures as the brickmaking family of Shaw; the oil, transport, and publishing interests of the Irvings; the Henson newspaper records; the fishing interests of Connors Bros.; the Marven baking entrepreneurs; and the records of major regional enterprises such as Bathurst Consolidated. New Brunswick's economic and business history is thus a field of great potential for archivist and historian alike.

In general, the business historian cannot expect to discover much by way of collections or published papers from local historical societies in Nova Scotia. The Nova Scotia Historical Society has published a fraction of the papers read before it since its inception in the 1870s; some of the rest may be found in summaries reported in the Halifax newspapers, or published in full in other contemporary journals such as the original *Acadiensis* of 1901–1908, or in the *Dalhousie Review*. In substance, however, few dealt with economic or business subjects beyond such related matters as currency, post office, transport, and privateering history — and virtually none was concerned with events beyond the Nova Scotia anti-Confederation flare-ups of the 1870s and 1880s. Only in the past two decades have a few articles appeared dealing in a sophisticated way with economics, imperial trade, and immigration. The Society has not attempted to establish a collection of original materials, partly no doubt because, unlike New Brunswick, Nova Scotia established a Provincial Archives in a handsome building on the campus of Dalhousie University some forty years ago.

The Archives of Nova Scotia has not, however, until very recently given particular attention to the acquisition of business materials. A recent and preliminary catalogue of Manuscript Group No. 3, "Business Papers," gives evidence of some useful holdings, however, and of greater promise for the future. Other transcript groups such as No. 6, "Industries," No. 7, "Ships and Shipping," and No. 18, "Railways" should be examined where appropriate. Unfortunately, Nova Scotia appears to be even further behind than New Brunswick in implementing an effective records management and archival depository programme for government records. Consequently, for the business historian of recent events, access to government materials concerning subventions, industrial estates terms, or other matters may pose some problems. Still, the Archivist, C. B. Fergusson, has recently affirmed a policy of encouraging the development of government records management, and of building the province's business archives; with a highly cooperative staff matching New Brunswick's two archives, the future seems brighter.

Among the Archives collections are many of the same types of governmental administrative, legal, and bankruptcy records to be found in the Fredericton Archives. In addition, some military and naval records have a particular significance for the port city of Halifax, and for the province as a whole. Most of the items listed in the "Business Papers" catalogue are slender groups of papers, widely scattered in respect to place and time and offering little prospect of company histories. Several others deserve special mention, however: the Zwicker collection, a vast and invaluable record of the Lunenburg fishing and West India trading company of Zwicker and Co. (1820–1939); the large collection of Nova Scotia Steel and Coal Corporation papers (1861–1969), an incomplete record and richest in the last quarter century; the Old Bridgeport [Coal] Mines papers (1869–1908), a more useful collection including nearly complete letter books; and the large, but still uncatalogued collection of the Nova Scotia Savings, Loan & Building Society (1853–1950). Among family papers, the most valuable are those of the South Shore lumber and pulp manufacturing firm of Edward Doran Davison & Sons, whose political activities offered an interesting counterpoint to their business operations in the last half of the nineteenth century. It is hoped that further discoveries, by filling in some gaps, will increase the usefulness to the business historian of the diffused character of the Archives' present catalogue.

Nova Scotia, too, has two principal archives for business historians. A few hundred yards from the Provincial Archives, Dalhousie University's Killam Library in 1969 established a Business Records Division under the immediate care of Charles Armour. This budding collection has been formally recognized by the Business Archives Council of Canada as a regional archive. An impressive early catalogue has been prepared, including materials rescued very recently from the perils of Halifax's current downtown redevelopment. Again many of the materials will only become useful when more records are discovered, but the declared policy of collecting business records offers great expectations. Among the best holdings are the records of several prominent Halifax firms: William Stairs Son & Morrow, records of this singularly important firm from 1879 to 1937; the tea manufacturing firm of J. E. Morse & Co. Ltd. (1871–1952); the papers of the Neptune Theatre Company; and the correspondence and design sheets of W. J. Roué, designer of the famous schooner *Bluenose*. Among the best from other parts of the province is an invaluable collection of the Weymouth family of Campbell, general merchants, shippers, lumberers, and marine insurers since the last quarter of the nineteenth century. This collection alone is an index of the regional ambitions and entrepreneurship of the small coastal towns of the Maritimes.

Maritime depositories alone cannot suffice the business historian. For example, in the archives of the Imperial Bank of Commerce in Toronto lie the records of several of the early Maritime banks; at the University of Toronto the papers of the Commerce's great president, Sir Edmund Walker, are invaluable. In the Public Archives of Canada at Ottawa are the papers of New Brunswick's Sir James Dunn, the long-time President of Algoma Steel Corp., Ltd.; the letterbooks of the general managers of that most aggressive bank in Upper Canadian-Maritime mergers, the Bank of Montreal; and the correspondence of such important Prime Ministers and Finance Ministers as Sir John A. Macdonald, Sir Charles Tupper, and Sir Leonard Tilley. At Greenwich, England, are the ship-brokerage records of C. W. Kellock & Co., whose associations with Canadian shippers of the 1850s were legion. Nor should the possibilities of developing an oral history record be overlooked. The field is open, but it is important to move quickly, to alert businessmen to the value of preserving records. It is also important that the principal archives in the Maritimes should establish policies of collection and cooperation. For local historical societies and boards of trade there arises a special opportunity in retrieving the record of the past and in working cooperatively with professional archivists and historians. But it is upon the latter, the professional historians, that the chief responsibility rests — as it is to them that the greatest opportunity opens.[22]

[22] My thanks for assistance are extended to the Provincial Archivists of the Maritimes and to their staffs, the Archivist and staff of the Archives Division, New Brunswick Provincial Museum, Charles Armour, Douglas Boylan, Harry Fleming, Ian McAllister, Dr. J. C. Medcof, Norman Morse, Robin Neil, Richard Wilbur, Glynis Wilson, and to Trent University for a summer research travel grant.